WILSON'S NIGHT THOUGHTS

BOOKS BY EDMUND WILSON

*I Thought of Daisy*
*Axel's Castle*
*The Triple Thinkers*
*To the Finland Station*
*The Wound and the Bow*
*The Shock of Recognition*
*Memoirs of Hecate County*
*Europe without Baedeker*
*Classics and Commercials*
*The Shores of Light*
*Five Plays*
*The Scrolls from the Dead Sea*
*Red, Black, Blond and Olive*
*A Piece of My Mind*
*The American Earthquake*
*Apologies to the Iroquois*
*Wilson's Night Thoughts*

# Night
# Thoughts
# by
# Edmund
# Wilson

*New York*

*Farrar, Straus and Cudahy*

# Contents

v

## POETS, FAREWELL!

## PARODY, SATIRE AND NONSENSE

## ELEGIES AND WAKEFUL NIGHTS

## STAMFORD

## PROSE OF THE THIRTIES

# THREE RELIQUES OF ANCIENT WESTERN POETRY, 1951

# A CHRISTMAS STOCKING, 1953

# A CHRISTMAS DELIRIUM, 1955

CONTENTS

THE WHITE SAND

1917-1919

# Southampton

*November, 1917*

Ah, English forests, delicate and fine!
   Ah, older England our encampments mar!
I coin, among your coppices of pine,
   A little gold for leaden days of war.

The tangled oak, the beech's slender bole,
   Make tracery against the morning's gray;
But what brave colors bank the hills that roll
   Where drift the leaves on Princeton paths to-day?

New Jersey forests! where November grieves
   To find her brightest fabrics blurred and blown,
More things are dead in Princeton than the leaves,
   Nor has your flaming beauty passed alone.

# Epitaphs

## I
### AMERICAN SOLDIERS

All sullen and obscene, they toiled in pain.
Go, countryman of theirs: they bought you pride:
Look to it the Republic leave not vain
The deaths of those who knew not why they died.

## II
### AMERICAN OFFICERS AND SOLDIERS
### WHO COMMITTED SUICIDE

What agony was yours whom here offend
These bitter graves? Turn not in scorn the face
From those who, breaking, fell before the end,
Nor yet from those whom base war rendered base.

## III
### A YOUNG GERMAN

Say never that the State concerns you not,
O Artists! though you toil not for your sons.
See where I lie—I and my paints forgot—
Whom Munich bred to fall by Essen's guns.

## IV
### A HOSPITAL NURSE

I, catching fevers that I could not quench,
When twenty died for two that we could save,
Was laid with dog-tagged soldiers in a trench,
      Glad of no meaner grave.

# New Ode to a Nightingale

*Base Hospital 6 at Vittel in the Vosges, June 8, 1918.*

Ah, why do you sing to me who cannot hear?
   Your foolish music leaves the night as dead
As do the stars of June, no longer near,
   Strewn meaningless and little overhead.

Sweeter it sounded through the poet's word,
   When, from another silence that was peace,
The Nephelococcugian flute I heard
   Or gazed with Christ above the groves of Greece,

For then those tones flung glowing to the dark
   Spoke summer's richness and the soul of June;
To-night the sharp lament of dogs that bark
   Can speak no less and yaps a fitter tune.

# Chaumont

*January,* 1919

Remembering the flowers my mother's hand uncloses
Between her hedges spread with spiders' laces:
Narcissi, pale and straight like April's rain,
The peony's deep stain,
Pansies with kittens' faces,
And summer roses,
Whose yellow lingers from the summer dawn—
Remembering how she loves the rabbits on the
　　lawn—
The barren desks and empty offices,
Where nothing wise is done,
Had nearly slipped my mind—
With all the deaf, the tongueless and the blind,
Whose works and servants thrive beneath the sun,
Unlovely and unkind!

# The New Patriotism

Assemblyman Theodore Roosevelt, chairman of the Legion's Americanism commission, called a meeting of that body to-day, at which it was decided to thoroughly Americanize all war veterans, then to utilize them in the work of making good citizens of the foreign-born of the State.—*The New York Tribune*, March 3, 1920.

Lieutenant-Colonel Roosevelt
Has unequivocally felt
That nothing less will now suffice
To purge the people's hearts of vice
And save Americans from schism
Than vigorous Americanism—
That newly found and certain cure,
That cult incomparably pure,
But only fully understood
By people who are wise and good,
Like Major-General Leonard Wood.

And through this faith he will inflame
The dull, the angry and the lame—
The men who only yesterday
Learned not to ask but to obey
And, netted in a narrow mesh,
Opposed the guns with living flesh.
This word will fire them to forget
The strands of that steel-woven net—
How they were bullied and inspected,
Court-martialled, censored and suspected;
How they said "sir" and snapped their hats

8

To save the world for democrats,
And how they suffered Hard-Boiled Smith
Lest liberty be made a myth.
And when their zeal begins to burn,
They, eager advocates in turn,
Will teach the Dago in his mine,
The Pole that stokes from nine to nine,
The Hunky in his sullen herd,
To love that one transcendent word,
Which heals all wounds, which opes all shops,
Which dazes Hunkies, Poles and Wops.

And then the sun will shine indeed,
The stars with greater calm proceed,
The plants perpetually ply,
Unvexed by treasonable sigh!
Production will have burgeoned so,
No honest man need ever go
Without his seven motor-cars,
His twenty kinds of peanut bars,
His fifty different sorts of hose,
His eighty makes of underclothes,
His morning dish of Shrivelled Rice—
And all for such a pleasant price—
And business will be very good,
And men will vote for Leonard Wood!

But what of those poor boys who died
Before they could be purified?—
Who never drank to toast the peace,
Nor had their holidays at Nice,

Nor climbed, bedevilled weary men,
The topless hill of Brest again,
Nor scarce believed the day had come
To lie on hard decks, going home?
Well, some are sprawling, deaf and blind,
In corners difficult to find—
By shattered barracks, trench and barn
Between the Argonne and the Marne;
And some are lying side by side,
More easily identified
By wooden crosses in a row—
But even those whose names we know
Cannot be reached in their position
By Colonel Roosevelt's commission.

—Yet stay! it never shall be said
Our care cannot redeem the dead!
Strike out from every epitaph
The kind of name that makes us laugh—
The Oles, Isidores and Fritzes,
The Mandelbaums and Meyrowitzes,
The Kellys, Kovalskys and Krauses,
Sciapellis, Swensons, Stanislauses—
And give us graves with every man
A certified American!—
A Smith, a Wood, a Ford, a Hill!
Our zeal shall save their honor still!—
Though they, detained in foreign spots,
Can never now be patriots,
But have, for all their sweat and pains,
These beds beneath the winter rains.

EUROPE

# To a Painter Going Abroad

Tell her I know the cold of northern hills
  But breeds intenser heat;
Tell her I know what desperate pastime fills
  The summer's slow defeat—

Cannes out of season not more desolate
  In sun than duller skies
Whereunder I remember, waking late,
  How far away she lies.

Paint her in green as once we saw her pierce
  The frosted smoke-fogged room
With beauty clear as ice, as fire fierce—
  And say to her I come.

Yet never now to travel toward Vittel!—
  South now to seek her, say!—
South, south, to that soft-graying Esterel
  That fades on rose and gray—

Lest, looking on the cold roads of Lorraine,
  Long trod, long brooded of,
Tears breaking for the fog, the frozen pane,
  Betray the eyes of love.

# Stucco and Stone

*To John Peale Bishop*

### I

By summer seas that lull your flight,
    For ever known and never old,
Some gleaming town of rose and white
    May yield you bodies rose and gold—

There where the waves are brought to heel,
    There where the Alps, no longer free,
Come down like elephants to kneel
    Beside the glazed and azure sea;

Or—parched for madder, rose and red—
    Where madder, rose and yellow rot:
Gay drooping palaces that wade
    Green waters ordurous and hot—

Such postures you may still provide
    As, throbbing the redoubled bout,
Murano's mirrors multiplied
    Above, below and all about.

### II

Yes, choose for youth the silver-tinselled night,
The mirror of the East that takes her hue;

But I, the dusky-toned, the dry, the brown,
But I, the city crowned with that clear light
Which roofs the streets with crystal white and blue
And cuts the cypress black above the town—

That beam intense which, biting the straight stone,
The low-domed hills, clipped sharp the cliffs of Hell,
That radiance divine and bright to blind
Which brims the valley, where a vision shone
That fled like snow before the lips could spell,
Or like the Sibyl's leaves before the wind!

### III

Florence or Nancy —Nancy nobly cold!—
Ah, still in dreams I ride again as once
Those northern roads, and late reënter there,
Below white August clouds with rounded bellies,
The great high thin-ribbed gates of black and gold,
And stand in the wide eighteenth-century square
Beneath stone urns that top gray-yellow fronts;
And drink the ecstasy of that dry air!—
—Yes: still I seek down vistas of Callot,
With yellow leaves along the linden alleys,
Old houses in a sober brass-trimmed row,
Leaf-freshened courts, clear windows long and low—
And those gray ancient gods
That bear about their battered empty pods
The eighteenth century on pose and face
In fresh indelible grace.

# The Lido

Rank with the flesh of man and beast,
The deep's obscure and fetid leas—
Old rotted cargoes from the East
Distilled to salt—the peacock seas
Breathe softly; sunken in its mold,
Drowsing in sand, the body bakes;
Sails of burnt orange and dull gold
Await the wind; a woman shakes
Sand from her shoe; all brown and bare—
One loose red gown for legs and breast
Fast ripened in Venetian air—
A girl plays ball nor stirs the rest
Of lounging bronzes by her feet;
White hats; pink peignoirs; yellow and blue;
The dry fierce steady beams that eat
The body.
              —Oh, I dream of you!
I see you stride the sandy bed,
Wide boy's eyes smiling with content,
Black-eyed, black-lashed, red-filleted—
I take you in the striped tent—
I strip you of your shining sheath,
Crowd wide your thighs with steady knee,
Stab flesh with flesh and sharply breathe,
Exhaled from open flanks, the sea.

16

# Boboli Gardens

There were no gardens there like those
That, groomed for pleasure and for ease,
Rose-clouded with the laurel-rose,
Hung high above blue distances.

There were no fountains, dolphin-fed,
For idle eyes to drift upon,
Where gold-fish, flecking green with red,
Drift idle in the eternal sun;

No sloping alleys gliding smooth
Through velvet glooms or golden light,
Round-moulded like the marble youth
That stops the alley-way with white;

No naiad satyr-sprayed and pale;
No lap-dog lions poised in rank;
No Ganymede, demure and frail,
The satyr crouching at his flank;

No Homer smooth on creamy skin,
With green-blue-gold embroidery lined.—
The black and dingy boards of Ginn
Your poets, like your God, confined.

In bare-swept houses, white and low;
High stony pastures never ploughed;

17

The pure thin air; the frozen snow;
And the sad autumn dark with cloud—

There, setting bare feet on bare wood,
They came who late in silks had gone;
Dim candor by your desks they stood,
Austere to wake the winter dawn.

# LESBIA

## Lesbia in Hell

When Lesbia came down to Hell,
Her lovers, feeling still the spell,
Flocked piteously about her path
And called her name in tears or wrath.
A broken company they stood,
All hacked and maimed and black with blood;
And one had lost his wits, and one
Was blind and blotted from the sun,
And one, with pain behind his eyes,
Went bleeding from between the thighs;
While women at their sides appeared,
Who gravely stared or sharply sneered
Or stood abashed, in quick despair,
Before the fire that lit her hair,
The noble throat thrown back so well,
The brow so bravely borne in Hell.

But Lesbia unregardful came,
Nor smiled nor spoke a single name;
But, soon arrived at Satan's throne,
In that strange dry and moving tone
Of hers, she spoke—and sorrow stirred
The tearless hearts of fiends that heard—
A sorrow never known before,
A sorrow deeper than Hell's floor.
"Lord Satan!" she began. " I come

By the gates of death to find a home.
I sue for freedom and content:
I could not feel your punishment!
Hell cannot match by force or art
The passionate and arid heart—
There is no jail in Hell for me
Like this that holds and will not free
The spirit virginal and fierce
That, soiled by love, befouled with tears,
In squalid prisons fluttering,
Still breaks the strain it cannot sing:
A music burning and serene,
A music somber without spleen,
Gay without laughter, white aglow,
Shedding the hottest lust like snow—
Founding like light in molten wind,
In blurless marble of the mind,
The spirit and its ecstasy!—
O Father Satan, set me free!"

Then Satan, as the silence fell:
"There is no setting free in Hell."

But Lesbia, lifting eyes so sad
They would have given all they had
To comfort her, yet could not speak
Their glow-worm words to anguish bleak
As winter fields, began again:
"O Satan, give me silence then!
Long have I dreamed among the wheels,
The screaming hounds that lap my heels,

Of silence, silence—to lie down
Untroubled by the bitter town,
The cruel hungry lips of lovers,
The hateful streets whereover hovers
The hawk aloft the vacant skies—
Forgetting these, to close my eyes
And sleep—and be unborn again,
Unlit by love, unlopped by pain—
A sightless being, deaf and dumb,
A buried stone, a sunken crumb
Of earth that cannot even weep.—
Oh, Father Satan, give me sleep!"

She ceased and watched the King of Hell.—
The rugged fellow pleased her well:
She liked his face—a little coarse
Perhaps, but full of life and force,
The eyes alight with lustihood,
The nose long, aquiline and good.
And as she watched she slightly smiled—
And Satan faltered like a child
When next he spoke. He said: "My dear,
You may learn yet to like us here.
With all eternity before you,
Why plead at once the place must bore you?
Before deciding what to do,
Endure a century or two;
Then, if you yearn for silence still—
Since I who cannot make can kill
(He lied, as we shall see: the Fiend
Cannot wipe out a soul that's weaned),

I'll send you beyond life and lover.
But meanwhile wait and think it over."

And while he spoke, an avid fire
Consumed all duties but desire—
He would have yielded trust and throne
To make her moistened mouth his own,
To bite her lips until they bled,
To crush her on a secret bed.
 Then—in a flash—he fled the thing
(For Satan is a moral king:
He must condemn on principle
 To fill the wide domain of Hell);
Snatched suddenly his eyes aside.
"We will not have her here!" he cried.
"That One whose triumph wrought our loss
Hangs bleeding from a harsher cross.
His plight makes Heaven desolate
For grief that, having found a mate
To drink His cup, His baptism share,
With him the cruel crown to bear
In that unneighbored pride of pain,
He prays and preaches now in vain,
Nor ever wins with wild desire
To share the inviolable fire.
Well may God damn her in His rage:
Fit goddess of a godless age—
Dismissing her, with callous grin,
To shake our very faith in Sin
And even plant—He knows it well!—
Fresh horns upon the fiends of Hell!

This alien on breeding bent
In both our countries discontent!
If we would save our kingdoms whole
We must beat down her harlot soul,
That she will neither guard nor sell—
Else we shall have no peace in Hell!
Destroy her then!"

                And straight a guard—
As soldiers, brooding peace and scarred,
Stay not but heed the stronger word,
As horses make blind leaps when spurred—
Stood forth; she shrank; and at a touch,
That Lesbia who had been so much
Was nothing live and nothing fair—
A bit of dust that staled the air—
The bright brow and the body round
A pinch of ashes on the ground.

And all the shades looked round again
And plainly saw that they were men,
Who, safely damned, beyond reproof,
Crept close below the narrow roof.
But the proud fiends forgot their pride—
The griefless fiends, who never cried,
Cried suddenly in piercing pain,
That so much beauty should be slain—
And then could only stand and stare,
As if their hearts had perished there.

But ash was shadow like the flesh:
    Their monarch has been mad and ill—
Walks out to brood, lies down to thresh.
    The soul Lord Satan cannot kill.

Shut out the square!—
Though not for grayness and the rainy path.—
For that intolerable aching air
Of meetings long resolved to silences
And absences like death—
For the throat a moment lifted, the wide brow
	shaken free,
Where there was neither leaf nor wind
A dryad by her tree—
Against the narrow door that closed the narrow
	hall,
Blank then but for a night that now for all
With blankness wounds the mind.

Gaze out with steady glare!
Present the tough unbroken glove!
For suddenly you heard to-night
Your voice that speaks and saw your hands that
	write,
Yet never speak nor write the name they
	love—
And knew the hours were waves that wash away
Farther each day to sea the summer sound
Of children shrill and late, of summer hours that
	run
Late, late, yet never sleep and never tire,

Before they meet the sun.
We spoke the sudden words, the words already
        known—
We spoke, and spoke no more, for tongues were
        fire.

Now, watching from this shore at last, alone,
I seem to wait the turning of that tide
That ebbs for ever.

                Children, waking to the day,
Cry out for joy.
                My stubborn heart to-night
Divines the fate of souls who have not died,
Buried in sullen shadows underground—
That reach forever toward the shores of light.

# Infection

Five days in fever thus I lay—
With stinging eyes could only stare
Where naked branches cracked the gray
Or fog suffused the empty air.

Baked like a crock, without, within,
By night I came to understand,
With shifting limbs and shrivelled skin,
Brunetto on the burning sand—

Yet him like some poor soldier gassed
Recalled—to shudder at the sign!—
Unslaked by poetry at last,
The pain but not the poet's line.

I thought, bad whiskey, manners, plays,
Bad talk abroad, bad work alone,
Bad damp apartments on bad days,
Have poisoned me from brain to bone—

These streets where once my freedom found
Love, summer and the muse—I start
To gaze upon that happy ground
With hatred and a sickened heart—

Yet knew—and deep in fever sunk—
Not fogs had stretched me there to sprawl,
Not all seen, said, read, written, drunk,
But the bad heart that poisons all.

# A Young Girl Indicted for Murder

All night the summer thunder that crashed, but
    never cracked
The prison of the smothered town,
Resounded, where I lay, about your prison bed,
To which one furious and drunken act
Had suddenly borne down
The spirit fierce, the stubborn copper head.

And all night, from the dull distended air,
The still unwetted empty street,
That company I kept oppressed me there:
Those praisers of the past, accepters of defeat,
The ghosts of poets—violent against God
No longer in my day; with men of thirty-odd
Fierce with the first resentments of their teens;
And those robuster captains of the age,
From brooding on some boorish heritage
Grown loud with sullen spleens.

I thought, those have foregone to carry arms;
And if these others, if a few,
Have struck, it was but drunkenly like you,
In desperate alarms—
Like you that for the butcher of your heart
Struck down your worshipper. And when have
    they—

So rash to shatter pain, with such swift passion
        wild,
Assailing lest they break—sustained a bitter part
With braver lies than you I watched to-day—
Pale, slender and a child,
Enduring without tears
The prison, the barbed "pen," the prosecutor's
        sneers?

—Now, all night long the summer thunder flaps
Above the town, above my bed, above
Your cramped repose of fear and festered love,
Repeating impotent claps.

# The Dark Room

Shut the windows, shut the door—
Never go there any more.
Stop the keyhole, pull the shade,
Hiding where the corpse is laid—
Locking in the leafless tomb
Of the close and darkened room
The corpse that blackens and grows
    rank,
Stiffened on the polished plank,
Beneath the ceiling clear and high
Where things that shine were not to
    die.

Seal the lock and let it be—
Stuff the crack and lose the key.
Though the air turn foul and thick,
It cannot leak to make you sick—
Leave it to its shuttered murk.
Make the servants do their work:
If you say nothing, they will stay,
Meals be served three times a day.

# Nightmare

And when they found the house was
    bare
The windows shuttered to the sun
They woke the panther with a stare
To finish what he had begun
To finish what he had begun
To claw the walls like webs of grass
To gulp the blinds that blanked the
    sun
Lay bare the panoplies of brass
And when the panther ate the brass
The walls the sun the house and all
They only watched the people pass
And lost their bleeding in the brawl
The house was gone
The light was out
The blood was spent
The panther dead
And oh the labyrinth destroyed
Swept like a cobweb overhead
Swept down and no more labyrinth.

# Provincetown

We never from the barren down,
    Beneath the silver lucent breast
Of drifting plume, gazed out to drown
    Where daylight whitens to the west.

Here never in this place I knew
    Such beauty by your side, such peace—
These skies that brightening imbue
    With dawn's delight the day's release.

Only, upon the barren beach,
    Beside the gray egg of a gull,
With that fixed look and fervent speech,
    You stopped and called it beautiful.

Lone as the voice that sped the word!—
    Gray-green as eyes that ate its round!—
The desert dropping of a bird,
    Bare-bedded in the sandy ground.

To-night, where clouds like foam are
      blown,
    I ride alone the surf of light—
As—even by my side—alone,
    That stony beauty burned your sight.

NEW JERSEY
AND
NEW YORK

# Highballs

*To John Amen*

### I

How many bright days blazing on the air,
Ice-highball-crystal-glazing through the glass,
Imbued with sunlight till the trees run sun,
Of Seabright or New Canaan, slow to pass,
Have passed, with all their fluid afternoon
For ever at flood-tide of trees green-gold—
With ocean's firm approach that blue vibrates
Some blithest final peace!

     The ice is ringing cold—
Say when—the amber mounts—the pitcher
  waits,
Dull luster of a silver nebula.

And we shall read the trees and try to say
What secret they convey—
Their green and gold against the solid light
Our fullest-hearted truth and farthest sight!

### II

Above the spacious lull, the happy lull,
Of late drinks drunk at leisure, gray and dull,
The city darkens for the summer storm—

In which a bell beginning seems to ring
The college classes with their nasal clangor,
Dragging us back to boyhood.

                              Brittle anchor!
We have left those friends to keep each other
        warm—
We float alone, serene above the swell—
We know the stars as they the proper streets—
We know the ports as they their appointed
        beats—
We know the channel, and those chimes that
        swing
Are but the buoy-bell!

# A Train Out of the Terminal

Late shrinking gold reflected in the panes
Of model factories. December. The gray
    afternoon.
The earth forsakes the regions of the sun,
And we turn each away—
Having learned to walk in houses as in streets,
Unwarmed by passers-by.
                      I dreamed to-day
Of those wild fishy-smelling little girls,
Naked in shreddy garments, brown as negroes,
    bred
By summer in the mud of Jersey beaches.

# To an Actress

## I

Doubt not, because in this bad town, my dear—
    Too shrewd for feeling and too quick for skill,
    Where even those who would do well do ill,
Through feebleness or ignorance or fear—
Those masters who can neither learn nor teach
    Pass by, not seeking even, the deep heart,
    The will that keeps it for the shapes of art,
The dark eyes and dark voice that give it
        speech—

Doubt not, where all seems doubtful as the
        dream
    Of some uncertain script which dirt be-
        grimes,
    Produced with borrowed money for a day—
Doubt not their lives, beside your playing, seem
    The badly spoken parts of frightened mimes;
    Yours the reality and theirs the play.

## II

And I who never doubted, yet have played
    The falsest parts in that ill-favored piece—
    Cold tenderness and trumped-up ecstasies—

42

How many times, remembering faith betrayed,
At thought of you alone through fault of mine,
    With loneliness and darkness all around—
    I've waked at night in horror and, half-
        drowned,
Spat bitterly as bathers choked by brine.

And I who once of truth and passion purled,
    I knew myself a liar from that day—
        The deep heart and its truth are all with
           you—
I knew it, though Broadway were all the
        world,
    Though I myself had helped to write the
        play,
        And coached the cast, and set my name
           thereto.

# American Masterpieces

*To Stark Young*

"Now you can drink all the coffee you like
and sleep like a child."
                                    Advertisement

In ignorance I longed for Grecian vases,
    Or even an Elizabethan skull!
Is it for this the prizes and the praises
    Rain down like buck-eyes, thudding thick
        and dull?
Behold the slogan! Passionate but Pure!
    Successful Treatment for the Poet's Curse!
Lee Wilson Dodd can look at literature
    And never sleep at night a wink the worse!
Academies shall crown the novelist
    Who, squeezing, makes a theme—as smooth
        as plush!—
Which might have broken Dostoevsky's wrist,
    Run out and lie like ribbon on the brush—
The play whose proper pressure might have tried
    The hard old veins of Sophocles to pump,
That takes us for a stabilated ride,
    The high catastrophe a padded bump—
The poet who does Dante, Yeats and Donne,
    Yet never seems to pale a shade less pink—
The crack biographer who points the gun,
    But only makes the acrid powder stink!
The critic buys the favor of the rest

44

By modelling their busts in vaseline.—
Our Comfort-Value is the Best by Test—
    The Heat Has Been Extracted from the Bean!


Alas, the great! They have lived, and lost their
        pains—
    They leave us harrowed, those unhappy men:
The reason labors and the spirit strains—
    How shall we ever bear the great again?—
They let us feel too much the surgeon's frown
    Intent above the bloody breach trepanned
In some poor brawling pauper's broken crown,
    Where logic holds the gorge and keeps the
        hand—
Or some tough soldier's tuned harmonica
    Playing against the ache from shin to knee—
Which makes his men remember—and grow
        gay—
    The bars and girls of home they'll never see.

# Copper and White

The blinds are down—so warm we lie—summer
    is coming—
Remote and rumorous the town—
Taxis, like raucous pigeons homing,
With grating gears arrest their flight,
And inarticulate children screech.
—We dream, my dear, we dream in vain to-
    night
Of lonely yellow sands and love at noon
On that wide open solitary beach—
Or, weary from the sea, outsleeping soon
Our weariness, of turning mute from sleep
To love, in darkness beaten by the deep,
Where happy lovers drown . . .
In vain we dream—for summer comes—the
    town is dumb—
And dumb almost the heart—
The splash of playing children makes a peace—
And muffled from some sleeping pond they
    start—
Quick-struck but dulled by dust and summer
    come—
Ripples of taxis scratching to release.
—So warm we lie—ah, now! and now! we meet,
All in our mouths—and now and now and
    now!—

46

I knew that passionate mouth in that pale skin
Would spread with such a moisture, let me in
To such a bareness of possessive flesh!—
I knew that fairest skin with city pallor faded,
With cigarettes and late electric light,
Would shield the fire to lash
The tired unblushing cheeks to burn as they did—
That mouth that musing seemed so thin,
Those cheeks that tired seemed so white!

—But now it is for us, the smell of summer kisses,
But now it is for us—
With this long soft enchainment of caresses,
Grown more precipitous—
And now we fall—all topples—steep for fear!—
All topples—tupping—pouring—and the
        pause! . . .
Ah, let me kiss your quiet mouth, my dear—
The room is quiet as it was!

—So now with what I lose refreshed they flow,
The reveries of love by friendship staled—
Of friends by love made hateful to each other—
Of love ill-met and broken so!
—We are so lately met wonder has never failed—
So soon to part we shall not see it go—
So happily met that neither knows the other!
—What anxious lovers, say—what bridegroom
        and what bride—
Have found all hope, all passion satisfied,
While still but a strange woman and strange man?

(To taste the cigaretty copper hair, to feel the fire
   from cheeks so wan!)

More slowly, slowly, now, with more deliberate
   play,
We move with summer's timeless tide again—
I close my eyes, you turn your face away—
The spirit cries with frail delicious pain . . .

Now sleep and numbness—we have love enough—
Sleep comes—and all the mind that feels
Is dull—dull and at end—we dream in vain to-
   night—
The fire that burns the cheeks from such a fairness
Wakes never now the fire that burned the mind!—
Sleep comes—the trucks go home—the summer
   numbness seals
The room and leaves us dim in all our bareness—
Dim on the daybed, tumbled warm and numb—
As warm and numb we seem as pillows left behind
In some apartment empty for the summer . . .
In moments such as those why must I speak of
   love? . . .
Sleep comes—in vain to dream . . .

# PROSE OF THE TWENTIES

# Jersey Coast

## A TRAIN'S WHISTLE

It moans—in the late afternoon, through the open countryside—unhuman, pressing and sad—intoning, a moment prolonged, a country of summer and sun from the vagueness of memory's verge: rank swamp rushes of Navesink with a yellow strip of sand for horizon—men sink crab-bait from motionless boats—high terraces, green and sheer, with white flagpoles over the river.—It moans—with wide lawns, summer cottages—we used to creep under the evergreens—a hammock—the *Dolly Dialogues* —young ladies with large white sleeves—young men who came down from town on the boat: *I've a tale I long to tell, sweet Marie!*—we were going for a picnic to Navesink—she was reading us the *Tanglewood Tales,* and when she came to where Hercules inquired, "Can you tell me, pretty maidens?" all the grown-ups began to laugh—her frank clear American laugh—it must have been to that note they made love.—It moans, and moaning swells, and howling hastes away, and fades in eager flight.

## II
### SWIMMING

Once outside the dry shadow of the bathhouse, we squint into white and fierce blue. The soft sand oozes drily from our toes and scorches our soles as we walk. Round blossoms of umbrellas confront us—awning-striped in white-and-green or melon-striped in red-and-yellow. Blue water floats red caps. Here we damp our feet where the sands have been darkened by the water; here we wade among silver nets. Blond stripling girls, in slips of red or green, with straight necks and slim straight legs tanned deeper than their bobbed tow-heads, insatiably jump the waves or toss tennis-balls on the beach—a boy with orange legs and arms slashes the blue with fast strokes. We melt in this heavy sun; and if we want to save our bodies, we must cast them like his in hard orange bronze—we must immerse them in this blue molten metal white-cold about our knees, which is yet not the statue but the mold. The climbing rim of the chill—a wave has stung us and wetted us—lie full-length, repose in the cold. Watery mountains swell to meet us—we can climb them. They shake their fraying crests—the world is all white light and water. Alongshore—white walls—the slim piers—sea-flapping flag—fragile and blurred—the silver fringe—to sea, the stems—the fishing-nets—their gray stems—the blue sea—bury face—in blue sea.

## III
### THE SUMMER HOTEL

A highball: ice fished from plain glass pitchers. Old-fashioned removable screens that brace the low window-sashes: outside, two late bathers looked out—dark suits and coral limbs—at the first cold blue, dashed already with the white-caps of fall—the first cold blue and the earlier dark, they speak already of the pressure of time, the waning of ambition, the disappointments of love!—the cycle of life that approaches its close with the cycle of the year.—A train wails beyond the hotel with all the sadness in its humble shriek of the stations it has still to stop at in its progress along the shore—Galilee, Long Branch, Elberon, Belmar, Avon-by-the-Sea—crumbling crazy hotels; soda-fountains boarded-up; cottages, incredibly flimsy, ready to capsize like sand-castles—Italian villas, Swiss chalets; manor-houses and mosques—umbrella-trees unadmired; unpolished garden globes; pergolas naked of vines; imperial lions and dogs drowned now in unweeded lawns.—All alive and fashionable once, in the rakish old racing days! George F. Baker, Lillian Russell, President Garfield, Jay Gould—"all the statesmen, all the big gamblers, all the actresses!"—a line of victorias that stretched all the way from the race-course to the shore—that race-course where the record was made for the run on a straight mile track, overgrown with ailanthus and locust now, where only the hoboes camp and the village boys take their girls. So nations have flourished and fallen—we wear them like our houses, our clothes—we cast them and leave them to rot. Lillian Russell goes elsewhere to-day and she bears a different name—Eastlake wears a different aspect—they are playing the races far away!—And this pale old yellow bureau, where the plain water-pitcher stands, and these shabby discolored red carpets in the long halls!—To hang behind among the husks of life, left alone with the melancholy of the shore!—to watch winter darken the sea, strip the beaches of bathers and close up the sea-bleached hotels—abandoned so long ago by the powerful and the gay!—I must find out tonight about trains! We must get them to bring us more ice!

# Oneida County Fair

*Upstate New York*

Crowding dense in the booth-lined lane, breathing foulness of food and humans—tramping the raw grounds, wadding boots with grass-matted gum—tough weather-rubbed girls in white stockings over ankles as thick as gate-posts, old women from lonely farms, squint-eyed, broken-toothed and bent—dowdy housewives, blond-haired farmhands, husky wide-mouthed little girls—idiots in pushed wheel-chairs, cripples with spider arms and legs—they buy twisted-wire jewelry and red glass beads—pay to see the Snake-Eater, the Wild Man, the Hermaphrodite Heifer—contribute to displays of burnt woodwork; goose-chase and log-cabin quilts; home-stuffed ground-hogs and owls; copies of old Gibson drawings; paintings of puppies in rope-frames; still-lifes of dead jack-rabbits and cantelope—they look on at slack trotting-races, at the inflation of a tarnished brown balloon—they stolidly take rides on the Merry-Go-Round, the Flying Swing, the Snap-the-Whip, to the calliope-blast of two alternating tunes—*If you knew Susie like I know Susie! Oh!—Oh!—Oh! what a girl!* —that intoxicate the glaring day——

Builders of strong stone houses to stand against the cold and the dark—ploughers of boulder-sown pastures—masters of the rolling waste, which the

thistles and mullein-stalks bristle—scrawled across
with low long stone fences that must perforce wan-
der with the slope, yet for an acre left ruddy with
buckwheat or gold with the débris of oats—drivers
of black and white cattle, where the cows repose in
august groves or graze high on the round bald moun-
tains that velvet their own sides with shadow—fishers
in evening ponds, when the sky leaks its last fluid
yellow and the air has grown dimmer than day only
as clear water is dimmer, where the heron hastes
flapping off and the bull-frog throbs in the dusk—
hunters by black Adirondack lakes in the night of
the dark North Woods, where the deer breaks her
covert and the black bear keeps his den, where the
great white violets rise from the leafage of a thousand
falls—bathers under ferny ledges where the jewel-
weed drips orange gouts, where the silver stairway of
rapids expands to the smooth dark pool—where the
voices of men in the silence sound as faint and as far
as birds—where the figures of men, like the crests of
the elms, like the hawks that range above them, like
the very high drifts of cloud, are lost in such a sky!

# TRANSLATIONS

## Death Warrant

Papini: *Basta coi verbi ladri e le parole sorde!*

Enough of words, so tawdry and so dull!
    Enough of literature, so florid and so faint!
We marketers of rouge to make earth beautiful—
    We only smear her granite with our paint!

Be silent and adore: these were the primal laws
    Of those rapt dwellers in the primal day—
Before the poets came with predatory paws
    To pillage earth and put her on display.

Like flowers pressed and classified and pent
    In some grand-duke's collection to crumble and
        to bleach,
The maiden riches of the world were spent
    Among the greasy pages of our speech.

The furnisher of desiccated graces,
    Between a cypress and a nightingale,
Intones a spell exceeding cracked in places
    For salvaging a muse exceeding stale.

With bathtub hurricanes and faded sunsets trailing,
    With alabaster heroes and stuffed leviathans,
We paste, with sighs and sweatings of oracles tra-
        vailing,
    The face of life with plaster of romance.

Enough of words! The poet must abjure!
   The poet must return with all his purples furled!
So may we, when at last we bury literature,
   In silence taste again the savor of the world!

# Dedication for a Book*

A. E. Housman: *Signa pruinosae variantia
luce cavernas*—

Those starry signs that freak with light
The frosty caverns of the night,
Sea-born and bright when daylight dies—
Together we have watched them rise,
Late wandering, where fields lay wide,
The lone and silent countryside.
So once, while still our place was blank,
The poet watched them where they sank,
Setting below the Latian sea;
And, mindful of mortality,
Earth-sprung nor spared from earth for long,
He looked aloft and launched his song
Against the everlasting stars—
Alas! to leave, with many scars,
A warning, all too plain, of odds
Which mock the man who trusts the gods.
For, though to Heaven dedicate,
With all the universe for freight,
His verses found misfortune fast,
And, washed upon our strand at last,
Shipwrecked and battered, blurred and lame,
They scarce can tell their maker's name.

* A translation of the Latin elegiacs prefixed by Housman to
his text of Manilius: "*Sodali meo, M. I. Iackson, harum lit-
terarum contemptori.*"

I have not plied, importunate,
The stars that harass human fate
Nor, begging guidance from above,
Besieged the gods, but, touched with love
Of mortal glory swift to fade,
Have sought renown through human aid
And, man, have chosen among men,
To stead no heaven-assailing pen,
A comrade, mortal-lived but stout,
Whose name shall bring my volume out.
—"O comrade," let me say, "whose name
May perish with my pages' fame,
Yet worthy through thine own to live:
From human hand to hand, I give—
To thee who followest away
Those rising signs to seek the day—
This present from a western shore:
Take it: to-morrow runs before,
With those whom life no longer owns
To lay our flesh and loose our bones—
To dumb with all-benumbing thrust
Our wits that wake not from the dust,
Nor spare, with learning's lettered leaf,
The bonds of fellowship as brief."

# The Night Attack

Petronius: *Lecto compositus vix prima silentia noctis—*

My limbs for rest I scarce prepare,
  To silence scarce resign my eyes,
When Love has laid me by the hair,
  And plucked me up, and bade me rise.
"My lazy servant! Last of churls!
  Behold," he cries, "your horrid plight!
You lover of a thousand girls,
  You lie with empty arms to-night!"
Outdoors, with flapping gown, I dash—
  With bare defenseless feet I stray—
In lagging haste, in sallies rash—
  Loath to return, ashamed to stay.
The traffic of the day is done,
  The sounds of dogs and men are dead—
I only fleeing—I alone—
  O mighty Love! the lonely bed.

# POETS, FAREWELL!

1929

When all the young were dying, I dwelt among the
    dead—
Many I lifted from the homeless bed
And laid in that low chamber side by side,
But they were unknown men,
Nor told me youth had died.

But you—when all the years of honor and success—
Skill, courage, learning, and their fullest scope
Had brought but darkness, brooding, loneliness;
The solitary walk, the muffled door;
Scorn of that public life which once had been your
    hope—
When dead I saw you, silent, straight and lean,
The film of age's tarnishment effaced,
Life's heaviness refined—
Looking, I knew at last that I had seen
That man of whom old Princeton teachers told—
The wonder of the Halls, the generous, the bold—
That youth by age and honor left behind,
By manhood's melancholy languished for—
The face of that young Princeton orator,
Rejoined in death at last.

—I blamed the day, the place,
Where flesh was rotting where it seemed most
    smooth,

Propping with age's comfort and grave ways
The broken back of youth:
Bred to one world and wearied by this other,
From which youth's straight backbone still kept you
    out,
You had earned but isolation and decay.

—Now I, more arrogant in a wiser day,
But half my life behind me, son of that father,
Know what blind life, what tomb of solitude,
What doubt, what draining of the spirit's blood,
Were ended where you lay.

Poets, farewell!—farewell, gay pastorals!
  Clear amber cider-brandy; green-eyed cats;
  Dim "blues"; blue willow-pattern dinner plates;
Waking to birds and light from three white walls;
Green deeps of ponds the sun-burned bather
      cleaves—
  Dark waters, warm by gusts or loded cold;
  Blue hills, green valleys like great maps unrolled;
Weeds in the garden; hornets in the eaves.


—We have rhymed under gray skies in the stubble
      grass—
  Sped plunging motor-rides with drunken song—
Had Wyatt with breakfast, Yeats with the final glass.
  —Poets, farewell!—O subtle and O strong!—
Voices, farewell!—the silver and the brass—
  I leave that speech to you who have the tongue.

Here where your blue bay's hook is half begun,
    I find you fled on those mad rounds you make—
    As if with sleepless demons on your track,
Yet lodging with the daughters of the sun—
Pursuing still that high romantic mood
    Through flight from love to love, from friend to
        friend;
    While she who dwells there sovereign to the end
Draws now her final strength from solitude.


—Yes, moored in a shadowy room I have seen that
    shape—
    Who once by sleepless winds herself was sped—
    She haunts me here in mind's and time's
        despite—
The last gray clouds and pale gold of the Cape—
    The scent of sweet-fern crushed beneath my tread,
      As once I smelt it through the smothered night.

—And you who faint at either's hard expense;
    Who idle and in exile almost grow
    That comfortable personage you show—
Almost persuaded by your own pretense—
Bred to one world and baffled by this other,
    Too poor for pride, too courtly for compliance—
    Did you and I once frame a late defiance
Against that world of desk and death, together?

—Old friend, fine poet—those romantic skies
    Have fallen—shall we harvest ray or flake?—
The very language of that vision lies.
    Yet who for doubt, for danger, may not quake—
Though all the darkness throng behind his eyes—
    Imagining a world his words must make?

✻

Dim screens obscure the dawn,
As dreams my senses clog—
Yet there the pale bright sun,
The dark trees dripping fog,

Make landscapes white and black:
Strange radiance, overhead—
Below, the molten lake
Of cold and silvered lead.

—O sun of opal ice!
Before your lens is sure—
Before your mists arise,
O waters and dark shore!—

Or ever graving blade
Of Evinrude have woke—
I shall have plunged and weighed
Dark waters with my stroke—

I shall stare round and see
That black receding brink—
Let breath and arms rise free
And all the body sink.

# PARODY, SATIRE AND
# NONSENSE

# Nocturne

*Impromptu to a Lady*

The foxes wink their onyx eyes;
The trancèd witches twitch their wigs;*
The pixies snap, like startled pies,
Their frozen filigree of twigs.†

Ice-sheeted crofts, close-hedged with thorn,
Confront Diana's dinted shield;
The watch-dog's bellowing, forlorn,
Chills sharper sharp-chilled stream and field.

Then rise! In some deep-sunken hole
Below the drifts you shall be kissed;
Or, crouching in some hollow bole,
Snow-cushioned for the winter tryst,

Cold bone shall ring against cold bone;
The skeleton like flint shall spark;
A high thin thrilling javelin tone
Shall glance like ice-beams on the dark—

---

* They were stirring in their sleep with dreams of an in-
describable character.
† The pixies construct little arbors of twigs to protect them
against the winter. These they thatch with leaves; but, at the
first breath of autumn, the leaves are blown away and the ill-
advised pixies left exposed. Many die.

75

Shall speed on stiff shrill-whirring wing,
An exquisite and crystal bird,
To where the guard that keeps the king
Stands heavy by his heavy sword—

Shall graze his ear, shall penetrate
To where the monarch heaves in sleep,
Close-shrouded by his curtains' weight,
Tight-walled with ramparts dense and deep—

Shall prick like lightning to the brain
And with a fierce electric flare
His skull shall burst with bristling pain
In fizzing fragments on the air!

# Quintilian

Quintilian walked on the Quirinal;
   Rome was crashing to decay;
The tilted shadows of the cypress
   Notched the Appian Way.
Quintilian, in mild elation,
Pondered a peroration.

Quintilian walked among the quince-buds;
   Roman order collapsed;
The catacombs beneath his tread
   Hid churches crudely apsed.
Quintilian, in a tempered glee,
Recalled a shrewd peripety.

Quintilian enjoyed the quince-buds,
   (Which he couldn't distinguish from peach);
He was brooding on asyndeton, astyanax,
   And other figures of speech.
Nero and his sycophants
Were violating their uncles and aunts.

Quintilian mused on a ruined quern;
   The barbarians gathered like thunder;
Nobody came to warn Quintilian
   To stand out from under.
The skies with triple bolts were torn

And hypermetric calves with seven feet were
    born.

The waters drove; the dyke burst;
    Quintilian was crushed like a quince—
Leaving nothing but his monumental works,
    Which nobody has read since.
—At least neither I nor John Bishop has yet,
Nor has anybody else in our set.

Alas! all things like shadows fly:
    Quintilian, Nero, Rome,
Quince-buds, asyndeton and I
    To dust and ash must come!
Yet suns still shine and quince-buds blow again
To light the loves and lives of other men.

# The Extravert of Walden Pond

To Betty Spencer, who said that somebody's statement that "Thoreau was a neuro" sounded like a song by Cole Porter.

A jumps-and-jitters fighter,
   As some of you may know,
Was the great American writer,
   Henry D. Thoreau.
He was skilled at making pencils
   And the neighbors bought his goods,
But he grabbed a few utensils
   And he vanished in the woods.

Oh, Thoreau was a neuro—
   Like us, you will admit.
He went without a bureau—
   It made him feel more fit.
He took to the forest with some soap, with
   A nickel's worth of nails and an axe—
Oh, how could he cope with
   Those early American fac's!
     He had a yen
     For Walden Glen—
The bushes and the rushes were his favorite den!
   Oh, Thoreau was a neuro!
   He liked Provincetown and Truro!
   Thoreau was a neuro, too!

He refused to pay his taxes
   And they put him in the cooler,
But he had his private axis—
   His undaunted animula.
He survived without commensals
   Where another man would break,
For he went on making pencils,
   Which he sharpened in the lake.

Oh, Thoreau was a neuro—
   Like us, I will repeat;
Yet it never made him pruro:
   His ideas remained sweet.
Tea was only tipple
   And he didn't know what hammocks were for;
But oh, how he loved to ripple the bosom of that
      water with an oar!
   He dipped his wand
   In Walden Pond—
He thought a sheet of water was a beautiful blonde!
   Oh Thoreau was a neuro!
   A noble old cuckooro!
   Thoreau was a neuro, too!

# Tannhäuser

*Inspired by the Arthurian poems of Edwin Arlington Robinson*

Tannhäuser, looking languidly away
From where the light fell gleaming on the ankles
Of young Bacchantes, who were troubled less
By any greater globe a man might lose
Than by the purple globes they dropped themselves,
Stared drily at the floor and bit his lip;
While Venus, frowning faintly, took his hand
And with a voice as soft as autumn leaves
And sweet as echoing of old regrets,
Began to question him as women do
Who falter to envisage what they see:
"Is this your tribute to my feast?" she said,
"To sit apart with such sad countenance
As makes me want to watch you every minute—
For fear the woven tissue of our days
(Which once could hold the passions in its woof
Of any knight or lansquenet or minstrel)
May suffer Time's erosion and wear thin,
In spite of all the needle-craft of one
Who shrinks to feel the losses that accrue
To wives whose eyes no longer hold their husbands
And goddesses who have no friends at court?"
"No tissue can hold long," said Tannhäuser
(And would not see the fingers that she stretched

With such a slow impingement of caress
Along his wrists), "No tissue can hold long
Of Venusberg or Venice nor can any
Who sees as far as you or I may do
See far enough to tell what sudden end
Of visible frustration or fulfilment
The gods may find to prestidigitate
From that tall hat of theirs, nor what long rains
Bring ruin to the little threads you weave
So deftly that they drive away old thoughts
Of azure skies and white Elizabeths
And leave me sighing that I see so far
Without the force to measure what I see,
A prey to most unconscionable qualms
And meditations."

               Whereupon she frowned
Less faintly by a shade and would have smiled:
"If I could find the road to what you see,
Inveterately indiscriminate
Of what you like to see or do not like
To see or what to see were straight to seek,
I'd weave a net to lay you by the heels.
And that's as far as I shall need to see."
And, petulantly tossing a gold curl,
She rose and led her dancing-girls away,
And Tannhäuser no longer heard about him
The little pattering of feet like rain,
But sat, still staring drily at the floor,
Alone among the stillness of old shadows.

"Were she to measure what I see," he mused,
"Or even half of half of what I know"—etc., etc.

*After three hundred pages, they part, without having arrived at an understanding.*

# The Omelet of A. MacLeish

1

And the mist: and the rain on West Rock:
    and the wind steady:
There were elms in that place: and graven
    inflexible laws:
Men of Yale: and the shudder of Tap Day;
    the need for a man to make headway

*MacLeish breaks an egg for his omelet.*

Winning a way through the door in the win-
    dowless walls:
And the poems that came easy and sweet
    with a blurring of Masefield
(The same that I later denied): a young
    man smooth but raw

Eliot alarmed me at first: but my later abase-
    ment:
And the clean sun of France: and the freak-
    ish but beautiful fashion:
Striped bathhouses bright on the sand: *Ana-
base* and *The Waste Land:*

*He puts plovers' eggs and truffles into his omelet.*

These and the *Cantos* of Pound: O how
    they came pat!
Nimble at other men's arts how I picked up
    the trick of it:

Rode it reposed on it drifted away on it:
   passing

Shores that lay dim in clear air: and the cries
   of affliction
Suave in somniferous rhythms: there was
   rain there and moons:
Leaves falling: and all of a flawless and hol-
   low felicity:

In that land there were summer and autumn *He slips*
   and nighttime and noon *in a few prizes for*
But all seemed alike: and the new-polished *philos-*
   planets by Einstein: *ophers.*
And a wind out of Valéry's graveyard but it
   never blew anything loose:

And the questions and
   questions
         questioning
            What am I? O
What shall I
   remember?
         O my people
               a pensive dismay
What have I left unsaid?
               Till the hearer cried:

"If only MacLeish could remember if only *The*
   could say it!" . . . *omelet be-*
And young girls came out: they were inno- *comes a national institution*
   cent strong in the tendons: *and gets*

85

*into Fanny Farmer.* Hungry for all that was new: and hearing
their eyelids were hazy with

Tears and delight: and the campuses brown
in November:
Ha but white shirt fronts pink faces: the
prizes won:
The celluloid tower with bold intonations
defended:

*He experiments with a new kind of peppercorn.* And the mean tang of Cummings turned
saltless and sleek on the tongue:
And a Dante gone limp: and a shimmer and
musical sound
That gleamed in the void and evoked appro-
bation and wonder
That the poet need not be a madman or
even a bounder.

## II

*He seems likely to lose his investment in his omelet.* And at last I drew close to a land dark with
fortifications:
Men shrieking outlandish reproaches till all
my blood tingled:
It was ragged and harsh there: they hated:
heart horribly quaked in me:

Then I thought "I have staved off the prick-
ing of many a sting,

86

These perchance I may placate too": I put
    in at that place:
I met them with scorn and good-natured
    agreement mingled:

Their fierce cries of "Aesthete!" and "Fas-
    cist!": and like them I railed at the
Bankers and builders of railroads: I said "So-
    cial Credit":
(He's a tough lad under the verse mister all
    the same!):

And the Polacks and Dagoes and Hunkies *He is obliged to reopen his omelet and put a little garlic in.*
    undoubtedly dead:
And behold these savage and sybarite-baiting
    strangers
Had many among them like me well-man-
    nered well-fed

Bubbling over with schoolboy heroics: their
    line had been changing:
And long in that plentiful land I dwelt
    honored in peace:
And then schoolboys from Britain came over
    us flying like angels:

Them too I courted: I labored to roughen *He is doomed to go on doc- toring his omelet.*
    the sweet
To stiffen the wilt of a style that seemed lax
    in that land:

A starch of Greek tragedy: stark Anglo-Saxon
the beat of it:

Stock-market talk: still my numbers as maw-
kishly ran:
(Señora, I could go on like this forever:
It is a strange thing to be an American):

I was wired for sound as I started again
down the river:
And my colons went out on the air to the
clang of a gong:
O when shall I ring with the perilous pain
and the fever?

A clean and clever lad
            who is doing
                  his best
                        to get on. . . .

# Bishop Praxed's Apology

## or *The Art of Thinking in Poetry* or
## *A Gospel of Falsity for an Age of Doubt*

A revelation vouchsafed me at about half past seven in the morning, in a state between sleeping and waking. I had had a discussion the day before with a non-believing friend of an older generation, who had been advocating a revival of religion.

And slowly answered Arthur from the bridge:
"The quality of mercy is not strained,
And God fulfills himself in many ways
Lest one good custom should corrupt the world.
Pray for my soul! more things are wrought by prayer
Than this world dreams of—wherefore let thy voice
Rise like a fountain for me night and day—
St. Praxed's always was the church for prayer
And mistresses with great smooth marbly limbs—
Thoughts never to be packed into a narrow act,
Fancies that burst from flowerbells and explode.
—If the red slayer thinks he slays
And if the potter's hand should falter at its task,
Say not, say not the struggle naught availeth—
Join hands, clap hands, for here comes Charley, hail
The ancient idol on its throne again,
The great Perhaps! . . .
God knows that I am with them in some ways!"

(*This shows the decline of religious faith, as typi-fied by Matthew Arnold.*)

# Disloyal Lines to an Alumnus

Who wrote poetry about coming back to college "like a man to his mother returning" and feeling "the keen swift faith that God is good," and who later complained in the *Alumni Weekly* that books by alumni authors were not being sufficiently praised by the reviews in that periodical.


I, too, have faked the glamor of gray towers,
I, too, have sung the ease of sultry hours—
Deep woods, sweet lanes, wide playing fields, smooth
     ponds
—Where clean boys train to sell their country's
     bonds.
Ah, high delights untasted by outsiders!
The Graduate College with its dreaming spiders!
May windows to the summer drunks flung wide!
The ivied peal of bells at eventide!
The drone of doves in immemorial trees,
The bumble of innumerable bees!—
And Beauty, Beauty, oozing everywhere
Like maple-sap from maples! Dreaming there,
I have sometimes stepped in Beauty on the street
And slipped, sustaining bruises blue but sweet,
And felt the keen swift faith, I will assert,
That God is fairly good to Struthers Burt!

—For God and Struthers Burt are gentle folks:
They differ from Jack Dempsey and Joe Doaks.
God is a big beneficent trustee,

Who asks well-bred professors in to tea;
Has swans and swimming-pools about the grounds;
Collects old clocks, and sometimes rides to hounds.
God was a club or two ahead of Burt,
But not enough to make him cold or curt—
They both believe in college comradeship,
Old college ways, the slow delicious drip
Of cool damp verse; and also, I suppose,
The keen and peevish tang of high-pitched prose.
Burt sometimes goes to stay with God for weeks
And utters fierce shrill Philadelphian squeaks.

# The Playwright in Paradise

*A Legend of the Beverly Hills*

What shining phantom folds its wings before us?
  What apparition, smiling yet remote?
Is this—so portly yet so lightly porous—
  The old friend who went West and never wrote?
That somber prince of wits, oppressed by Evil,
  Who made the rafters ring with insolent patter,
The floors quake with temblores of upheaval,
  The windows rattle to the tumbrils clatter?
The same, but born anew and better dressed;
  He has outsoared the shadow of our night;
We cannot clasp again the hand we pressed;
  Our anxious tasks are senseless in his sight;
We cannot speak to him.

                          Yet we must listen.
"Beyond the mountains lies the sea," he breathes,
  "Where billows, blue and brineless, glide and
        glisten—
  And there we dance in bougainvillea wreaths,
Speeding the golden day with golden shoes;
  Or idle in an innocent collapse,
With music and the lucent orange juice,
  While avocadoes drop into our laps.
We talk of glory—who glows brightest, least;
  And tell our gains, in decimals most dear

—And yet our riches may not reach the East,
    But fade like fairy gold at the frontier.


"We know that what we make is fair and good—
    From furrowed thought and sternest effort wrung.
—And yet to you who are not of our blood,
    Our very language seems a goblin tongue;
Our passions make you sleep or make you sick;
    Our characters are cookies cut from dough;
Our cunning plots, pure theorems of technique,
    Look all alike, and work you only woe.
Blind lead to you our glazing diamond prisms:
    A perfect pratfall[1] delicately placed;
A weenie[2] won through countless cataclysms;
    A dash of glamorous French muff [3] made chaste;
All history galloped as a gallant twosome,
    Designed with daring gag[4] and dainty drehdel,[5]
With many a big take,[6] grand oh,[7] high gruesome:[8]
    A king in mufti and a cottage mädel!
To see the life of music as a crooner
    Who loves a queen of song and doubts his future,
Dismayed by Continental goona-goona,[9]
    But rescued by his native ouchimagoocha![10]
To see the principles of Truth and Right
    Embodied in Paul Muni with a beard;
The toiling masses and their touching plight,
    Paul Muni with his chin and cheekbones smeared!


"You mock our paradoxes—you are rash!
    Our blessed dogmas make us free, though
        fettered—

Great Communists who only work for cash;
    Great stylists spelling 'cat' for the unlettered;
These and the great directors, Titans tenser
    Than straining whippers, dreamers of bold scope—
Submissive to a medieval censor,
    A Mr. Breen commended by the Pope.

"—And now the supervisor calls," he cried.
    "I must away!"

                    He left us in a breath;
And that bright specter seemed to turn a dried
    Cadaver in the golden air of death.

**1** *Pratfall:* full-length cropper, theoretically on the rear. Groucho Marx and his blonde topple and crash on the dance-floor.

**2** *Weenie: dénouement.* The Girl has sworn she will marry a Navy man; the Boy has been deprived of his commission for lovable insubordination. He retrieves it through an amazing feat of bravery and makes it possible for her to keep her vow.

**3** *Muff:* the feminine element. An example of the achievement mentioned is the sequence in which Danielle Darrieux and Douglas Fairbanks, Jr., spend a night in a hunting lodge together without offending the Legion of Decency.

**4** *Gag:* a joke, a comic device, usually acted out. The Bengal Lancer plays his flute, and a cobra comes out from under the bed and sways in rhythm to the music, thereby causing much mirth in the Mess.

**5** *Drehdel* (from the German *drehen*): an unexpected twist to a plot. Edward G. Robinson instructs his henchman to give the hero some knock-out drops; but, to the surprise of the audience, the admirable young man continues to fight Robinson fiercely. The accomplice has gone over to the hero's side.

**6** *Big take:* strong emotional response to a situation. The Frankenstein monster sees that his buddy has been killed and goes mad with grief and rage. He *takes it big.*

**7** *Grand oh:* extreme surprise. Maurice Chevalier is kissing the French maid when his wife comes into the room. They turn around and see her.

**8** *High gruesome:* hair-raising drop from a great height. Harold Lloyd falls off the roof of an office building and only saves himself by grabbing the flagpole.

**9** *Goona-goona:* erotic carryings-on. Derived from a picture about the love life of the brassièreless inhabitants of Bali.

**10** *Ouchimagoocha:* Spanish or Mexican love-making, with hot-blooded exlamations.

# ELEGIES AND WAKEFUL
## NIGHTS

# Night in May

This is the zero hour—all troubles and all blurs—
The will is lulled and falters, the dog desire stirs.
Here on the spacious daïs where I seem to lie in
    state:
Pineapple-pronged four-poster of a Utica great-great—
Here where the straining ages, the minds that contra-
    dict,
Fusing varicolored fires, make no tumult of conflict:
Ripe calf, pale yellow, India thin, rubbed parchment,
    boards black, blue—
I lie awake and long for you, and that is all I do.


—Yet I went there once in winter. Like a faded
    photograph,
The trees were streaked with yellow. The town was
    cracked in half;
The cops were on the Common; the Reds were in
    the pen;
The mills in all their squareness were squatting on
    the men,
To the croaks of death's-head houses in discolored
    grays and browns.
It was one of those damned squint-windowed grit
    and brick New England towns.
And I—I saw it plain as brick; how each his path
    fulfills—

The masters to the churches, the workers to the
mills;
The masters to four-poster beds, the workers to the
cold.
November sped October—the strike was five weeks
old;
I heard the pickets groaning in the dismal misty
dawn;
The pickets called me over; the patrolman moved me
on.
I went again in summer—among those enemies:
The trees were dark with August, the moon was in the
trees.
We had the house—Oh, whitest skin! dark, proud
and smiling eyes—
An Irish queen!—the first right moon I've ever
known to rise!—
Full moon—all free and sudden love—so much
forgot so fast—
Dark long girl's hair—like boyhood's hopes turned
real so late, at last!
We laughed together, dearest tongue, all tangled in
the bed—
You asked me what they'd had to eat and mused on
all I said.
But when I rapped the attic roof—still fearful for
your sin
You winced lest Mrs. Lipperkins might crisply cry,
"Come in!"—
And when I faced the fields again, now cold as au-
tumn grown,

How bright the moon! how moist the grass! but I was
  there alone.
For you were with the masters, and I had claimed the
  mill—
These tears we weep tonight will dry—these dews the
  nights distil—
So lock the windows, darling, and drive the last bolt
  home
And go to sleep and dream of me—the zero hour has
  come—
The kids and Mrs. Lipperkins will waken with the
  day.
—And yet you leave them open wide—it's I who go
  away.


But now we sutlers of the faith make such a shadow
  bout—
Such slaps and squeals and snarlings as never yet rang
  out
Since the gray trolls fought the gray trolls for the
  fattest rind of cheese:
While Mrs. Lipper, safe in church, bedevils you at
  ease,
Myself and Louis Leftwich, we do little for the
  mill. . . .
This is the zero hour—let the mind sleep with the
  will:
  Lie over, and lie still.

# Riverton

Here am I among elms again—ah, look
How, high above low windows hung with white,
Dark on white dwellings, rooted among rock,
They rise like iron ribs that pillar night!
The stars are high again; the night is clear;
The bed rolls with the old uneven floor;
The air is still again—I lie and hear
The river always falling at the door.

—O elms! O river! aid me at this turn—
Their passing makes my late imperative:
They flicker now who frightfully did burn,
And I must tell their beauty while I live.
Changing their grace as water in its flight,
And gone like water; give me then the art,
Firm as night-frozen ice found silver-bright,
That holds the splendor though the days depart.

# A House of the Eighties

No more in dreams as once it draws me there,
All fungus-grown and sunken in damp ground—
No more as once when waking I gazed down
On elms like water-weeds in moonlit air
Or heard the August downpour with its dull full
    sound—
Drenched hedges and the hillside and the night,
The largest house in sight—
And thought it sunken out of time or drowned
As hulks in Newark Bay are soaked and slowly
    drown.

—The ugly stained-glass window on the stair,
Dark-panelled dining-room, the guinea fowls' fierce
    clack,
The great gray cat that on the oven slept—
My father's study with its books and birds,
His scornful tone, his eighteenth-century words,
His green door sealed with baize
—Today I travel back
To find again that one fixed point he kept
And left me for the day
In which this other world of theirs grows dank,
    decays,
And founders and goes down.

# The Voice

*On a Friend in a Sanitarium*

All Virgil's idyls end in sunsets; pale
With death, the past of Dante opens deep;
The men of Shakespeare do not break, they fail;
And Joyce's dreamers always drift asleep.

—Her loved American laughter, male and clear,
That rang so young in London or in Rome—
A quarter-century gone, my fortieth year—
Is mute among those living ghosts at home.

And I who have been among them and who know
The spirit shrunken to its shuttered cell,
Now hear no laughter—only, piercing low,
This voice that always says, "Farewell! sleep well!"

———

I heard it, dulled with love against your breast,
I heard it in our peace of summer suns;
I heard it where the long waves of the West
Retard the dark with loud suspended guns;

And even in the white bark of that wood,
Those mountains roped and broken by our race,
Beside those high streams where the horses stood
And watched our strange and desperate embrace.

This blue world with its high wide sky of islands!
Pale cliffs, white cubes, the slender point, the little
    bay—
And over there, beyond the outer shore,
Its wildness and its silence,
Old kegs and beams of wrecks embedded in hot
    snows,
Will sink in awful lavender and rose
The red sea-faring sun—
This freedom of the sands, and summer new begun!

—But oh, my dear, among those dunes we lay,
And all the paths we left are drifted smooth
And we shall make no more!—
And death lies underneath
That cuts the world away.

Poured full of thin gold sun, September—houses
  white and bare—
Red salvia and yellow sunflower on the gray boards
  and pale air—
The village hush, dim children in the Sunday after-
  noon—
The insects in the straw-dry grass with their dry in-
  cessant cry:
Day, night, I sleep among them, wake to find them
  . . . So sat I,
In youth and long ago, before a book, alone,
Hearing the country afternoon, the dogs in back
  dirt-streets . . .
        But now all this—
Peace, brightness, the browned page, the crickets in
  the grass—
Is but a crust that stretches thin and taut by which
  I pass
    Above the loud abyss.

# Provincetown, 1936

Fat-pronged starfish, oyster-fed,
That slow on spirit fingers slide;
Snails in plump blue folds that spread
Purple feet below the tide;

Crabs that, humped in stolen homes,
Fence from doors they cannot lock;
Polyps budded pink, like wombs,
Filamented to the rock;

Sand-dabs sandside up in pools,
That slip in bat-flights from the hand;
Tiny mackerel trapped in twinkling schools;
The little silver eels that dive into the sand—

Mussels with broken hinges, sea crabs lopped
Of legs, black razor-clams split double, dried
Sea-dollars, limpets chivied loose and dropped
Like stranded dories rolling on their side:

They lose their juice and stiffen in the sun:
The tide that shrinks has shed them like a scurf;
The tide that floods will stir with waves that stun
Frail shapes that crush before the faintest surf.

Dawns, dawns, that split with light
    These tight and tarnished streets,
Dividing blinds drawn tight,
    Displaying livid sheets—

You flood the window-ledge,
    Yet here in mind and heart
Light enters harder than the mason's wedge
    That thrusts the rock apart.

After writing,
Reading late,
Too tired and tense
To take the author's sense,
My mind a metronome
That keeps its proper beat,
Always starting and alighting,
I strive to mark as if it were my own
The other's pulse too stuttering and slow,
To pull his periods straight,
To stretch them tighter than the vibrant bow
That speeds the arrow home.

✻

The crows of March are barking in the wood
Alarmed they haarch-haarch and yar-yar-yar
They have their exits and their entrances
And one crow in his life plays several parts
One crow mounts guaard-guaard in a tree
Gives yar-yar-yarning: all the parts are plain.
So once in these sparse woods before the dark
All lonely, wild and lyric twanged their calling.
At morning now who sleepless long have lain,
Loveless, nervous, tired, torn,
Almost I envy sentinel and sleeping host
Almost I envy voices grown coarse-coarse that caw
      the morn.

# Home to Town: Two Highballs

### First Highball

—My dear, whenever I hear anybody whistling in the
   streets at night,
I know it—darling, darling—that I'm of the city, too!
And those women are all provincials, the full-
   bosomed, the robust—
They are peasants beside you!—
The slim pale body and the blue-veined wrists—
For you and I are at home in the narrow room,
Between the jail and the river at the foot of the
   street, gray, glum,
And the El that accelerates, grates, shrieks, dimin-
   ishes, swishing, with such pain—
To talk the quick city tongue!
To talk to the one who knows!—
You and I shall be gone,
Dear, when the city goes!—
And all the city loves, intense and faint like you—
The little drooping breasts, the cigarettes,
The little cunning shadow between the narrow
   thighs.
They will get rid of cities—
They will make themselves better bodies—
But they will never have a girl so pale and blue-veined
   and quick and passionate as you—

111

—When I don't see you, dear,
The blood in my head sings like birds!—
The only singing birds we ever hear . . .
You watched some city sparrows the winter you were
    sick,
In the little backyard in Brooklyn when the snow
    was on the ground—
You fed them crumbs but you never could catch
    them at it.

## The Woman, the War Veteran
## and the Bear

Bill Gage adored his gay-eyed mate,
   The wildest girl in West Medill.
He took her driving fast and late,
   And married her without her will.
He dreamed adventure, dull at home,
   Adored her for the flights she dared;
She took him, fearing worse might come,
   One autumn she was sick and scared.


And then he had his wheels to watch,
   And she an empty house to fill;
The rains would come; the records scratch;
   And there they were in West Medill.
He was a heavy engineer;
   Her friends no longer sought her out.
She held him close and called him "dear,"
   And left him in distressing doubt.


She couldn't stand his sister's clothes
   And wouldn't go to see his aunt;
She telephoned her former beaux
   While Bill was prisoned at the plant
—And then the bugle blew; and Bill,
   Resolved to rouse her to romance,

Submitted to be set to drill
    And dressed and armed and sent to France.

And soon Bill's aunt and sister wrote
    That Annabel had played the scamp,
When Bill was scarce aboard the boat,
    With officers still safe in camp.
Bill took it out on flesh he jabbed,
    Amid the screaming and the smell!
He shot, grenaded, slugged and stabbed,
    And left his legs at St. Mihiel—

Then, fitted with a rolling stand,
    Returned in quiet, took his gun,
And stopped two lovers with the hand
    He'd learned to lift against the Hun.
Bill's arms were strong, and no one knew
    The skill with which he'd crept and swung.
A cripple was suspect to few,
    And those who wondered held their tongue.

Then Bill, this finished, turned his mind
    To learn to walk on wooden pegs;
Well-jointed, plausibly designed,
    He came to use them like his legs.
He took a harsh and sharp delight
    In kicking bricks and garbage pails,
In wading icy brooks at night,
    In pounding up his socks with nails.

And while Bill roamed the music halls,
    Alone on dismal pleasure hunts,

One night he found wild animals
   Reluctantly performing stunts.
"This bear," the trainer cried, "is fierce
   As any creature ever trapped!"
He banged his lash about her ears
   Till Polly lunged and snarled and snapped.

"The man who goes inside her cage,
   He gets a thousand dollars down!"
Bill stood up tall, approached the stage.
   The people took him for a clown:
The boys began to leer and laugh.
   But Bill was wrestling with the bear!—
He downed her while she clawed his calf,
   Amazed at flesh she couldn't tear.

The house went wild. The trainer pressed
   To take Bill on; Bill took him up.
And twice a day, from East to West,
   He played with Polly like a pup.
He'd goad her on, and wink and grin
   While all the house sat deathly still;
Then drink the loud ensuing din.
   It was a happy time for Bill.

And then the bear gave up one day:
   She shrank and held her head aside
When Bill came bounding in to play;
   Declined her meals, grew dull and died.
His act was off; and life was queer.
   He found the brute had been a mate.

He'd fought and fed her for a year;
    And now was frightened by her fate.

He saw her in her tight-barred box,
    Dragged from dark cars to blinding lights,
With endless jerks and jolts and knocks
    By beasts who couldn't feel her bites.
And Bill beheld unroofed abysses
    Which left him feeling black and ill,
Recalling ineffective kisses
    And helpless days in West Medill.

Now Bill detached his wooden half
    And set himself to learn trapeze:
He had his arms, and they were tough;
    He didn't need his feet and knees.
While people marveled underneath,
    A springing, sparkling, whirling speck,
Bill flew with elbows, hands and teeth—
    And missed and fell and broke his neck.

———

Bill earned not-being thus perhaps;
But here the moral seems to lapse.
Fame, neither accurate nor fair,
Makes Bill the martyr of the air:
Wherever from the brimming heart
Trapeze-performers praise their art,
He leaps among their topmost names,
His figure flanks their mirror-frames;
While Polly, now but pelt and bone,

116

Unnamed, unpictured, left alone
   By some waste siding in the sticks,
Lies under the wild burs and mullein,
That can't convey, though coarse and sullen,
   She still resents her master's tricks.

My dear, you burn with bright green eyes
   That shine like jewels of the mind,
Where clearest gazings crystallize,
   Translucent to the light behind—
   Let not those lovely eyes go blind!

In these divided darkened days:
   For when they darken and they fade
To turbid blues or duller grays,
   As cities mask their lamps, afraid,
   The very dawn is dimmer made.

# On Editing Scott Fitzgerald's Papers

Scott, your last fragments I arrange tonight,
Assigning commas, setting accents right,
As once I punctuated, spelled and trimmed
When, passing in a Princeton spring—how dimmed
By this damned quarter-century and more!—
You left your *Shadow Laurels* at my door.
That was a drama webbed of dreams: the scene
A shimmering beglamored bluish-green
Soiled Paris wineshop; the sad hero one
Who loved applause but had his life alone;
Who fed on drink for weeks; forgot to eat,
"Worked feverishly," nourished on defeat
A lyric pride, and lent a lyric voice
To all the tongueless knavish tavern-boys,
The liquor-ridden, the illiterate;
Got stabbed one midnight by a tavern mate—
Betrayed, but self-betrayed by stealthy sins—
And faded to the sound of violins.

Tonight, in this dark long Atlantic gale,
I set in order such another tale,
While tons of wind that take the world for scope
Rock blackened waters where marauders grope
Our blue and bathed-in Massachusetts ocean;
The Cape shakes with the depth-bomb's dumbed
    concussion;

119

And guns can interrupt me in these rooms,
Where now I seek to breathe again the fumes
Of iridescent drinking-dens, retrace
The bright hotels, regain the eager pace
You tell of. . . . Scott, the bright hotels turn bleak;
The pace limps or stamps; the wines are weak;
The horns and violins come faint tonight.
A rim of darkness that devours light
Runs like the wall of flame that eats the land;
Blood, brain and labor pour into the sand;
And here, among our comrades of the trade,
Some buzz like husks, some stammer, much afraid,
Some mellowly give tongue and join the drag
Like hounds that bay the bounding anise-bag,
Some swallow darkness and sit hunched and dull,
The stunned beast's stupor in the monkey-skull.

I climbed, a quarter-century and more
Played out, my college steps, unlatched my door,
And, creature strange to college, found you there:
The pale skin, hard green eyes, and yellow hair—
Intently pinching out before a glass
Some pimples bred by parties at the Nass;
Nor did you stop abashed, thus pocked and blotched,
But kept on peering while I stood and watched.
Tonight, from days more distant now, we find,
Than holidays in France were, left behind,
Than spring of graduation from the fall
That saw us grubbing below City Hall,
Through storm and darkness, Time's contrary stream,

There glides amazingly your mirror's beam—
To bring before me still, glazed mirror-wise,
The glitter of the hard and emerald eyes.
The cornea tough, the aqueous chamber cold,
Those glassy optic bulbs that globe and hold—
They pass their image on to what they mint,
To blue ice or green buds attune their tint
And leave us, to turn over, iris-fired,
Not the great Ritz-sized diamond you desired
But jewels in a handful, lying loose:
Flawed amethysts; the moonstone's milky blues;
Chill blues of pale transparent tourmaline;
Opals of shifty yellow, chartreuse green,
Wherein a vein vermilion flees and flickers—
Tight phials of the spirit's light mixed liquors;
Some tinsel zircons, common turquoise; but
Two emeralds, green and lucid, one half-cut,
One cut consummately—both take their place
In Letters' most expensive Cartier case.
And there I have set them out for final show,
And come to the task's dead-end, and dread to know
Those eyes struck dark, dissolving in a wrecked
And darkened world, that gleam of intellect
That spilled into the spectrum of tune, taste,
Scent, color, living speech, is gone, is lost;
And we must dwell among the ragged stumps,
With owls digesting mice to dismal lumps
Of skin and gristle, monkeys scared by thunder,
Great buzzards that descend to grab the plunder.
And I, your scraps and sketches sifting yet,

Can never thus revive one sapphire jet,
However close I look, however late,
But only spell and point and punctuate.

*February, 1942.*

# STAMFORD

These funny muffled woods; the rusted stream
Scarce rustling in the hollow; stifled weather;
An airplane dimly humming; dull as March—
In summer warmth the darkling light of autumn;
The very colors of the wood subdued.

   You are alone—
The woods are dumb with the dead.

The days and nights—pressure and relief—
    Outlast them both—wake till the snow is white—
Desire pales and dies—that heat is brief—
    The day was here like night—outlast the night!

For only when distaste and lust, and bright and
        dark—
    Silence and noise, the quiet and the quick—
Are spent against the will like waves, the rock, the
        Ark,
    Survives the surf that laps the crumbled brick.

Now the garage shows green—the servant wakes—
    My mistress sleeps—she dreams of nothing now—
But I, my thoughts stay while all the ground shakes.

    —My dear,
            My dear, you cough in your sleep—
    You say you gave me rock and ark, and I had for-
        gotten how.

# Birth and Death of Summer

### 1

These nights of silence before April breaks
The woods are dumb yet confident and calm,
We feel the firmness of the mounting month
And drift feet-foremost down the stream of time . . .
Warmer outside but still the wind moans . . .
A sudden buzz, the peepers' piping, wakes,
The tiniest moths, the slowest snakes, emerge
The green brushed in with more white flowers
    out . . .
Dumfounding moonlight of the mists of May
On dimmed familiar ground
The deep unreal valley green and gray
The something that it seems to mean and ask:
The musk of whiskey making us a mask
Nightlong we gaze moon-dazed . . .
With one hot day of haze the summer comes
The ferns that looked so fresh are suddenly lush
The lilies-of-the-valley lose their lustre
The sun is late, the light is later now
Great wooded mountains grow the gray old hills
Day fades and leaves its cold and lovely leas
And leaves us with the fading afterlight
You think of the cold fish in the dark streams
Their yellow bellies darkened by the water
The little bluish folded butterflies

The fox with blinking eyes:
The full and silent night.


2

The crickets and the goldenrod arrive together . . .
To fall asleep on sunken afternoons
Of rain and summer's ebbing in the green rank wood
Or humid summer nights that hum toward autumn
    now . . .
Red leaves, the sudden smell of fermentation
The leaves are falling in the tennis court
The court is pocked, the balls dull plop
And now the bright the blinding summer sports
The ruddy backs of tan, white shoes, white shorts
Are darkened by the gray air overhead
Among the towering trees that tarnished soon
The depths of chlorophyl so soon to be discolored
The haze of August turned to autumn mists
And sudden pathos twists with the quick wrist
The ball that leaps the backstop to the wood
—As if cool drinks at noon were ever true!
As if the cold had ever been to seek!
The cold, the cold again
Alone it makes us speak
With pathos and with pain.

# The Good Neighbor

Dense traffic, frequent gas, brick blocks,
A plant that manufactures locks—
Then sudden woodland, roads grown dim
With grass and branch, a broken stream
Resounding in a rocky glade:
Old farms gone back from share and spade
To birch and fir—a pretty bit.
And Mr. Pritchard rented it,
And rented an old pleasant house,
And bought a station-car, some cows,
A green-house, and a weather-glass,
All fine degrees and shining brass;
And patched the trees with trespass signs,
Which threatened folks with fearful fines;
And now the Pritchards sit and stew
And tell the farmer what to do.

Spring stirs the wood; the crows arrive;
Stems start among dead leaves alive.
But Mr. P. is stirred to wrath
To meet a couple in the path
That lurks along the stream, long known
To couples who would walk alone.
He tries a hoarse unheeded cough,
Then sharply shoos the culprits off.

—Now buried creeps the sweet arbutus;
The ferns unfurl like children's shooters;
Gray snakes, their doze of winter done,
Uncoil, still dull, to feel the sun;
The greasy brown and green of bogs
Leaps into life as little frogs—
Pokes up the rank and speckled hood;
Wild purple iris in the wood
And windflowers white whose roots ooze blood.
—The Pritchards go to much expense
To fix a stiff forbidding fence,
With snarling barbs. They never dream
Two legs can wade across a stream.
Yet lo!—one day they stop and stare:
A dago picnic sprawling there,
With oranges and cheese and wine.
They hadn't understood the sign!
(Early they rose and labored late
Such clever locks to fabricate
As guarded Mr. Pritchard's gate.)
So Mr. P., to make them stop,
Puts up No Trespassing in wop.

The summer trees shake down the rain;
The June-bugs bang against the pane;
The lonely moccasins expand
Their purple, veined and phallic gland.
—And Mrs. Pritchard, blithely dressed,
    Of undisturbed dominion sure,
Displays her duchy to a guest,
    A school-mate who has married poor;

130

When, horror! suddenly they see
A mattress spread beneath a tree.
What caterwauling, spitting, spite!
She had it burned that very night,
And watched it burn, and gasped and quivered,
And went to bed all faint and fevered.

And so while summer floods the wood,
The phoebe crams her crowded brood,
The tree-frogs pipe in ponds and swamps,
The moon-green moths assail the lamps,
The chipmunk winks among the stones,
And all the forest throngs and drones
With comfortable undertones—
The Pritchards simply concentrate
On keeping people off the estate.

—And now a hideous thing appears:
For gradually with the years,
They keener, fiercer grow—in short,
They come to love it like a sport;
And, all unknowingly, they lay
Deliberate traps to take their prey.
They let the careful fences fall;
They leave a ladder by the wall;
They let the trespass signs grow faded
In hopes their pheasants may be raided;
They disregard a broken bar
To lure the fisherman too far.
And Mr. Pritchard haunts the stream

Where high-school youngsters come to swim—
Keeps back till they are quite undressed,
Observes brown legs and swelling breast;
Then, feeding a ferocious glow,
He makes them grab their clothes and go;
While Mrs. P. extends the chase
In many mad ingenious ways:
By calls, complaints and wild alarms.
She sniffs for pigs on neighbors' farms;
She harks for revellers; she looks
For signs of sewage in the brooks.
If anybody's dog is found
Abroad on Mrs. Pritchard's ground,
She drags it promptly to the pound.
And so, by constant strife and strain,
Keeps neighbors, courts and cops insane.

A lively girl, who loved to blast
    Her beaux with snub and snort and snoot,
At twenty-nine she crowned at last
    Poor Harry Pritchard's patient suit.
—Sorrento, angry with the guide;
    The heat of Rome—an aching head;
The stench of Venice' tepid tide;
    Milano—all alone—in bed.
Poor Harry, with his weather-glass,
His peaches and petunias,
Has never dreamed, to hear her scold,
That she, poor thing, like him feels sold.
He used to think her not quite kind;
But, always timid of mankind,

He's learned at last to hate them, too;
And now he shares her point of view.

—O beaters of the winds that blow!
O damned that hate the happy so!
O dying who must nag and drive
To feel yourselves at least alive;
Who quicken with the kick that spurs
The victim's cry, the fighter's curse;
Who think your hired houses castles,
With valid moats and loyal vassals—
When human bodies, strong and bare,
Still swim your stream; when school-boys wear
Their diamonds in your meadow-grass;
Where paths keep fresh where lovers pass;
Where planes, for whom estates are splotches
By which they set their western watches,
Outsoar, outroar, outthreaten you,
And all your sulky retinue!
—Poor nights that veronal allays!
Poor frenzied rage on vacant days!
Poor souls so famished and so shrill,
Cold, crippled, cruel, crazed and ill!—
They starve like you; like you they strain—
Those lives you pine for but to pain;
Yet come to claim the season's good
As sure as summer to the wood.

## November Ride

The horse bends her head
In a bold homeward hope;
With stooped wolfish tread
The dog trots a rope.

Brown leaves all beneath;
The gray-bristling ridge;
Bare twigs in the path;
The stream breaks by the bridge.

—The stream in day clear
Looks suddenly bleak:
The last of the year!
The end of the week!

Just before the white blast—
Just before the dull mists . . .
The people at last
Are less than the beasts—

Yet you who have slipped
With me out of doors:
Brown-eyed, rapid-stepped,
Like dog and like horse—

For you womankind
Have cast forest and pelt,

Have contrived and designed,
Put on bodice and belt—

And you run with me still
In the stones and the cold
Till all I can feel
Is for round and for gold—

Gold white, gold red, round arms, rose-dotted breasts,
That long space between hip and knee, the striding
    thighs,
The vase-line of the throat that answers to the waist's,
The great round-lidded, heavy-curtained eyes;

The short dear feet that firm the perfect line,
Red ringletted gold hair that harbors hidden angers,
White skin like goldleaf beaten smooth and fine,
Soft as the goldsmith's chamois to the fingers—

        . . . Back home—dark now—
        High eaves—hard light—
        Dogs bark far
        On dark farms—
        Hard now—blank tonight!

The grass brown, the bushes dry:
The hidden brook ran green and high,
Wild ducks rose flapping in a rush.
  I walked the shrivelled woods and said:
"My steps disturb the winter hush—
  I am alive, and he is dead."

The morning bleak, the day gray:
The light was lemon off the bay,
The sands were needle-blown and bare.
  I trod the heavy hills and said:
"I still can taste the ocean air—
  I am alive, and she is dead.

"—I am alive, and they are dead.
  Yet, slothful and perverse, I slight,
Between the bottle and the bed,
  Dull morning and tormented night,
  This little work that buys the light."

PROSE OF THE THIRTIES

# Word-Fetishism

## *or Sick in Four Languages in Odessa*

To interpose the screen of a text between oneself and experience:

Books of the Oxford Press, tapestried with hand-woven verse or crammed to the margin with prose, the good full value of the British, in volumes like well-made boxes; German in thorny black-letter, like gratings of thick iron grillwork, or German of Insel Verlag, so admirably blocked on long pages, the masses of agglutinated language, emphatic with their primer capitals, held suspended in a margin of white; H. L. Mencken's square-ended Americanisms, coupled with hyphens like freight-cars, that nevertheless look so toothsome impaled on their careful pins; French of the *Grands Ecrivains de la France*, distinct to the thinnest serif, as elegant and strong as a Paris balcony, with the accents struck on as smartly as the tilt of a Paris hat—French that keeps dry on the greasiest paper, firm in the flimsiest binding, whose paragraphs lie so lightly on the pages only waiting for one to pick them up; the garlands in ropes of Italian prose, elaborately and slowly festooned, with the pronouns dangling down from the ends of the verbs, as ornate as a Renaissance ceiling; *v*'s for *u*'s of terse Latin verses, cut like inscriptions in brass, on stiff paper edged with gold; Latin prose, packed as solid as the bricks of which it was said that

Augustus left them marble; Greek of the sixteenth
century, all curlicues and crosses and dots, the com-
mentary as deep as mud; Greek of the seventeenth
century, still ligatured but running like a ribbon of
lace that is crocheted with the delicacy of the parti-
cles, the inspissated hem of commentary a little in-
terpenetrated with light; Greek and Latin on opposite
pages of a Villoisin *Daphnis and Chloe*, the Greek
curled in tight little scrolls, the Latin long *a*'s flying
accents, the old text of learning touched now with the
charm of the flowery meads it revives; and Greek of
the English editions, restored to its original severity,
gracious and spare and clear, and printed on India
paper; Russian with its Greek of the barbarian
reaches, with its blunderings and its Scythian hiss-
ings: books of the old spelling, their word-ends
weighted down by "hard signs," and studded with
strange bristling vowels like ornaments in a Byzantine
church, or Russian of the state-owned presses that
tries to move unencumbered, with its participles that
buzz like bees, its *zhe*'s that vibrate like butterflies,
its prickly tsar-crested *tse*'s—Russian forbidding and
tender, laconic yet quivering with life, poured out
for men and women who have just learned to read,
as fast as they can found the type, into formless gray
pages with no titles; and the good old nourish-
ing fodder of our home-grown American books,
brought out perhaps on shiny paper from somebody's
newspaper office or printed by the author himself,
with the rectangles of plain pale type all wall-eyed on
the facing pages; newspapers supplying quick lunches

from their trailing and flavorless columns; the fine dense grain that is binned in the columns of encyclopædias—

To put between oneself and experience the defense of a language, of words.

Ah, the pleasures of approaching a new language! The words are all at drill in the grammar. They are odd or attractive objects, curiously colored or marked; they become for us familiar little beings, with faces and tails and prankish disguises. They involve us in no moral judgments and they are devoid of emotional connotation: we can play with them like pets or toys. Then, when first we begin to see into their meanings, with what freshness the world reappears to us! Trees and tables, dogs, women and children, coming and going, God, government and butter, have assumed a new strangeness and interest, as if they were being named for the first time. And still for awhile the illusion persists: we seem to gaze through a blurring gauze on a stage excitingly lighted, at characters in picturesque costumes, who give voice to ideas and passions of an order different from our own.—But, as we watch, the gauze fades away: we find ourselves looking point-blank and in plain daylight at people just like the rest—they are putting the same food into their mouths, discharging briefly the same sexual desires, propelling themselves along the same roads over the same round and limited earth and under the same empty sky, for the same immediate ends, with the same aimless musings, as ourselves. They are saying the same things in their language that all the other human beings we have known have been saying in all of theirs.—And the work is where it was before, the ground is no better cleared, the plans are no further advanced! We lose time, we cry, with these screens and veils! The languages, all language, is a source of confusion! We must blow it away, beat it down!

—I was ill; and they were swarming over my mind like ants. I watched them running to and fro; I wondered out of what dark burrows—of history and pre-history—they had come. I noted derivations, resemblances; and I tried to round them up in groups, to string them on the threads of principles. But like atoms of soot they rose in the air. Was our envelope of atmosphere not clouded with them?—were not all the words that had ever been uttered hanging there like a fetid fog? Did we not breathe them and did they not asphyxiate us?—did people not fall down like drunkards, loaded with too many words?—And now I had words like a vexatious disease—they were multiplying inside me as bacteria—they were crawling in all directions, the words of all the languages mingling and barely for a moment seeming to shape as a phrase or some irrelevant fragment of a sentence. They were taking possession of my mind when awake, of my dreams when I dropped off to sleep. They were compelling me to focus upon them, isolating them as under a microscope. And the more closely I scrutinized these words, the more uncomfortably I came to realize that none of them had any meaning!

# The Moon in a Dream

Ten years or more ago I made the acquaintance of an American painter whose work I had never seen. I knew that he was a distinguished artist, and the quality of his personality stirred me to speculations as to what his pictures might be like. One night I had a vivid dream in which I thought I was looking at one of his paintings. This vision, as I found out later, was rather different from his actual productions: there was a mystery quite alien to his pictures; but it did have certain things in common with them, an objectivity, a stillness, a clarity. In any case, it has remained with me ever since almost as if it had been a real painting.

We are inside a small country store which has been shut up for the night. Outside the full moon is shining. The front window of the store, which is horizontal and divided into six panes, takes up a large part of the picture and, as it were, presents a picture inside the picture. To the left, within the shadowy brown of the darkened but moonlit room, we see the end of the counter and above it the half-shadowed shelves. The moon is somewhat right of center of the middle pane of the upper row. In the foreground outside are bare branches, showing distinct and brown, of trees that stand just out of sight on either side of the window—and, beyond, the empty fields of a

143

countryside, with small masses of bushes and hedges, which the moonlight confuses with their shadows. It is winter or very late fall.

The moon is round and bright in a moonlit blue midnight sky. The whole thing is a balancing of this brightness and blue with the dullness and brownness of the store. There is nothing strange to be seen, yet the picture is strange in an enchanted way. For one thing, it takes us into a solitude such as in real life we cannot know. There is nobody inside the store: it has been locked up till morning; and there is nobody to be seen outside. The solitude and silence of this closed-in place is something which nobody has ever experienced and which yet we are somehow experiencing—the solitude of being somewhere without oneself and of losing oneself with amazed delight in the serenity, the clarity, the mystery, the depth, of the moonlight, the countryside, the blue, which are seen through the panes of the window of the plain and abandoned room. Now that we are there with the moonlight, now that we are where no one is, we recognize the power of its beauty, which, measured and confined by the window, still, neutralizing all that is common, floods and transmutes the frame. We can never understand this beauty: we can only look and look at the picture, as if some thirst we had had were being satisfied without ever being sated— as we can never make out precisely what is out there in the moonlit fields. There is something more there than the fields themselves, but it is not a human

144

presence, nor is it something that has been humanly contrived.

But the painter has been here in the locked-up store, and he has seen what there was no one to see, and now he himself has not been here.

# Variations on a Landscape

## I

Going down to New York from New Jersey one day,
I fell asleep on the train. When I woke up, the after-
noon was late, and though the day still seemed full
and luminous, it held already the tragic suggestion
of the encroachments of the winter darkness which
each evening was clipping it closer. My mind was
still vague; I looked out: an infinitely spacious sky
with a disorder of autumn light, and below it, swim-
ming slowly past, a high lawn which was partly
masked by a hedge very thick and dark and from be-
hind which a scattering of tall lean trees lifted ragged
just-rusting crests. I had a glimpse of a square
brown house, rather impressive but empty-looking,
which slipped behind the train out of sight as I
was feeling the spell of the trees. For the trees and
the hedge seemed familiar: they evoked for me the
ground from which they rose: an irregularly-planted
lawn with slopes unplaned and paths well-worn;
and on this lawn I saw a company of children whose
universe was bounded by the hedge. I was among
them: I must have known them well, for, with no
conscious effort of imagination, I had peopled this
unseen place with them. They were all sisters and
brothers and cousins or something of the sort; and
the girls and boys played together on absolutely equal

146

terms. The girls had on, I thought, white dresses, and their hair was a little wild—they may all have been going barefoot.

I tried to think where I had known these children. At Seabright? The lawns there were ironed smooth. There had been fresh white tennis balls and rackets screwed-up in frames that meant serious business at the Tennis Club. In the background were quiet little girls who spoke intimate French to their governesses. And at night, when we were talking in bed, the automobiles on the Rumson Road rushed by with an exciting recurrent light. Or had it been in Charlottesville? The children were wilder there, but there was something like gallantry between boys and girls. The families seemed more demoralized, but in the midst of the demoralization there was a certain irrepressible arrogance. We would range through the campus at night—the Rotunda, in which the skeletons of prehistoric animals were grinning with great fangs in the darkness—the shadowy white colonnades in which the professors lived—peeking in at low windows where our elders were dining and drinking claret or at the basement of the medical school where the stiffs were laid out in the dark. Or had it been some summer in upstate New York? But no boulders in the landscape of my vision. No enormous elms. No evenings of lucent orange, aloft in the first Adirondack hills. No fragrance of cows from the pastures with its coarse underflavor of dung. Or had I caught some remote suggestion of the freedom of the middle Northwest, of children I had long ago seen but never had lived among? These children of my vision were surrounded by a vastness but it was not quite the Michigan vastness, not the purple of Michigan marshes, rank with the red-veined pitcher plant, flecked with gentians in the August grass like little blue tongues of flame. I could not identify my vision with any of these specific places, yet the landscape and the carefree children had something in common with all of them and might in some sense have represented them. It was perhaps that they had something American.

House and trees had now been reabsorbed in the capacious afternoon—afternoon would be absorbed by night. If I had been able, in my moment of vision, to look more closely about me, what precisely should I have seen in that place? An uneven croquet ground, perhaps, with chickens straying among the wickets. A hammock washed pale by the rain. The children would go in to dinner and afterwards play casino, or they would read Horatio Alger and Louisa M. Alcott, or they would sit around the fire and roast chestnuts when the somber autumn darkness had rendered the croquet-wickets treacherous, restored to the poultry and the familiar trees a certain independent strangeness and made the hedge a mysterious boundary like the Hercules pillars of home. Now the countryside stretched all about them, farther than it did by day, with waste fields and straggling trees, with occasional estates party cleared for islands of landscape-gardening, and solitary self-sufficient dwellings—farm-houses or half-farmlike or half-boxlike—of families so remote from one another that the children could not hear one another's shouting.

So it would not be the croquet and the chickens that were the essential elements of my vision: it was the relation of the children to the landscape, to that wide formless countryside, to those trees that rose rusting and weedy against the October sky. But was the relation necessarily to a countryside? Did the vision not have also its connections with some memory of city children?

I remembered an old house on West Fourteenth Street, in passing which, a few years before, I had had a somewhat similar illusion. It was a large brownstone mansion which, though tarnished by time to a dismal and rubbishy color, had stood its ground through the decades when all those blocks were being filled by small shops, and which now, in the otherwise unbroken expanse of dinginess, ugliness and cheapness, displayed starkly a stately magnificence. The basement had iron-grated windows and it rose above the sidewalk so high that the big door looked down on Fourteenth Street from a point of vantage almost ducal. The panels of the dark door were carved in rosettes and garlands, and this door was framed deeply in an elaborate entrance which had a stone-scrolled pediment above it and fluted acanthus-wreathed columns. On either side of this doorway were two tall windows with smaller pediments that opened on a gray stone-railed balcony, and inside one saw long folding blinds, white panels threaded with gold. Behind was a low old-fashioned stable, with a frieze of pigeonholes, in which the pigeons still seemed to be breeding, and hairpin-shaped double doors, which sometimes stood open and showed carriages that dated from some period when New York was half a provincial town. There was a decrepit and respectable old man, who still worked about the place, but who had come, like everything else, to look rubbishy. The lawn had gone partially bald and did not seem to be supplying much nourishment for miserable iris-plants; and on the other side of the house, the yard was very narrow and walled in by a block of shops. Here there was no grass at all, but only the dirt, hard and bare and strewn with bits of paper and glass; here only the thin skeletons of trees were leaning like overgrown weeds. But two bulging brown oriel windows protruded in the direction of these trees, and I imagined, very much as I was later to do in connection with that house in the country, a family of city children looking down from the security of their window-seats into the rainy April yard.

Were these children myself and my cousins? Was I reminded by this house on West Fourteenth Street of the old house on East Forty-First Street, just opposite where the Public Library was long ago beginning to be built and prevented you from going through to Sixth Avenue, the house where the dark-

oak dining-room was so richly yet metallicly deco-
rated with the dies of William Morris's wallpaper,
where we used to lose ourselves in the library over
Phiz's dark pictures for Dickens or manage surrepti-
tious dips into the case histories of Havelock Ellis,
then a series of grim brownish volumes available
only to doctors? Those children I had thus imagined
had something in common with us, and what had
they had in common with the children I imagined in
New Jersey? Why, those children in the house in the
city had had the spaces around them, too. The city
expanded, unfolded, and the houses moved or melted
away. The wallpaper patterns of William Morris
were no longer on Forty-First Street; the house on
Fourteenth Street had had no children, and no old
people either. The high flight of steps that led up to
the door was walled-in with a screen of stone which
reached from the pavement to the level of the sill.
The family had lifted their drawbridge, locked their
doors and bolted their windows; but they themselves
were dispersed in the spaces.

In New York, although New York was so much
bigger, it was just as it had been in an American
town, just as it had been in a western city. I thought
of a boy on a bicycle returning through the streets
in the late afternoon, his school-books strapped to
his handle-bars, and inscribing the curves of long
thoughts in the leaf-padded gutters of autumn—of
a boy I had once seen in Pittsburgh in one of *their*
boxlike houses, which was blackened by soot and,
like the house on Fourteenth Street, had evidently

been abandoned by its original owners—a boy in an upstairs window, dangling his legs from the window-sill and with his back against the frame, doing his homework in a sweater. Those raw constructions of wood and stone, those earth-scorching metallurgic engines which we had brought to the American wastes, must have seemed to a boy in Pittsburgh bleaker and more forbidding than the darkening skies of winter that opened, after all, on the great northern lakes and the Appalachian mountains and the Ohio flowing south, that opened away to the West, and to which he might look out from his perch for some lifting and far vista of the spirit.

### III

And I remembered now another glimpse which I had had from this same New Jersey train-window: the ball-park at Newark, empty and raw, beneath an apocalyptic sky, in which the November sun, pale, cold and clearly-minted, was dropping like the sun of the first days of Creation into the gray and illimitable waters of an engraving by Gustave Doré—an engraving in *Paradise Lost*, which as a child used to chill and depress me when I had had to pass the time in a boring house in which an old couple lived on whom my mother sometimes called.

Was there, then—*Paradise Lost* and Doré—some element, in my vision of the children, of that special romantic grandeur, a grandeur domesticated and turbid, which I had found in nineteenth-century pictures and which was stimulated by certain skies. The children and their trees and their house had a relation, too, to something else—to Doré and to all those old pictures.

One saw it in the Provincetown Museum in the big print of Boston Harbor that dated from 1857: the city steel-silvery on the water beneath the gigantic but clearing clouds of one of those Scriptural heavens—the steely needles of the church-spires and masts, the as yet so rare tall smoking chimneys, the domed State House, the docks raying out from the town, the square-rigged ships in the harbor, the old-fashioned side-paddle steamboats, the men and boys in queer long breeches and tall hats like truncated cones. But the gloom of the wharf and the fishermen's boats, the fish-baskets and the floating barrel, remind us of the Thames of Rogue Riderhood, those dark and muddy chapters of Dickens; and, above, there is that somber zone which stains and streaks the water, that somberness of the nineteenth century which goes curiously and yet quite appropriately with the innocence of the men and boys who have been out in the fishing-boats.

Of all the American country it is Boston perhaps that today seems the tightest, the most contracted, the most self-sufficing community. Yet even here, toward the sea and toward the hinterland, one still has a sense of the amplitude in which Beacon Hill is set, as one also feels this amplitude in engravings, where the subject is political or military. One feels it with the orator addressing the Senate in a wide and formal chamber of which even the nearest reaches are lost as in the dust and darkness of an enormous old-fashioned barn and where the shafts of motey light from windows one cannot see throw into relief in the audience a few white foreheads and collars, leaving the ladies who watch from the gallery infinitely dim and remote; one feels it in an incident of the Civil War: the general on the silken-flanked horse and with the beautiful spy-glass of a steel engraving, the soldiers of the Union army breaking up the railroad with picks, and the faces of the fugitive Negroes carved out also with a classical dignity, but the whole scene enveloped in a smoke-fog that spreads from the burning farms, that obscures the sparse stars of the flag and blots out the stretch of country and the limitless sky—that wilderness of the countryside again, which, elaborated, low and confused, extends away and away. In this vastness the war will be drowned with all the horror of its massacres and the strain of its marches and in spite of the long train it has lit—just as the unexplored immensities outside, for all the close personalities of the Senate, seem present under the Capitol dome.

And yet, is this all but a rhetorical mode—since it has brought to my mind Doré—which has nothing specifically American, a mode which had already been exploited to flatter Napoleon and Pitt before it was borrowed for Sherman and Clay?

IV

Have I ever received, I now ask myself, from a European painting or print any impression of precisely the same kind as those that have just merged in my revery with my feeling of the atmosphere of the household which seemed to slip by me on the train?

Aren't the landscapes of Church and Inness, in one of which might perfectly well have been situated that house and those children and those trees—aren't these landscapes in certain ways quite different from anything by the English or French? The colors and masses of Turner are *constructed* like a solid British palace: they achieve their obscurity and grandeur through thickening rather than expansion. The dimness of Corot is an exquisite dimness—and not far behind the birches in the mist are the turrets and grills of the gray château. But American grandeur and dimness are neither allegorical nor elegant: they are natural, almost homely. They are simply a place in which people live and in which they live a great way apart.

Have I not seen those children of my vision astray in Europe itself and did they not carry their landscape with them?

I was climbing the long hill to Langres in the summer of 1918 and looking up toward gray roofs and black ramparts from which a row of gargoyles jutted. As I approached, what I had taken for a gargoyle, something poised on a squat round tower that was lodged in the old wall, became plain as a human figure. It was an American soldier who perched there, chin in hand and elbow on knee, the black shape of his bent limbs and campaign hat cut out sharply above the stone goblins. They, with time-blunted jaws and dead eyes, hung to the wall like fungi; but the boy was a human and an alien, sitting there all alone and looking out on the fields of Champagne in the direction of a huge queer statue, the figure of the Virgin of Langres, set up by the grateful Langrois, after the war of 1870, to commemorate her intervention in saving them from the Germans. But those threadbare fields, those eroded hills, those towns that seemed sunk in their soil, that uncanny and awkward monument, were not what he seemed to be seeing. He had climbed up there, like the boy in Pittsburgh, to dominate a wide stretch of country, and in his eyes were the horizons of home.

# At Laurelwood

## 1939

I

Our grandmother lived in Laurelwood, and our parents used to send us to stay with her when they went away to Florida or Europe, or somebody had appendicitis.

This experience was always delightful. Our grandmother engendered about her a singular amenity and brightness. The essence of it seemed to reside in the exquisite odor of her house: the fresh fragrance of flowers combined with the seasoned smell of oriental rugs. Whenever I catch a whiff of anything however faintly like it, I am pulled back to that floor of childhood: the polished and slippery hardwood surface, the enigmatic pattern of the rug, whose warm and unfaded reds matched the colors of the dinnertime fire, and—one met it on an upper level— the shining mahogany table that reflected the row of books like a lake. After dinner we would fold away the brass wicker-wire fire-screen and supervise the progress of the blazing logs with the brass-handled tongs and poker; our maiden aunt, sitting before them, with her skirt folded back over her knees, would dramatize the crumbling red grottoes and send flights of elves up the chimney by giving the logs a hard knock. Above, in the shadow of the mantelpiece, stood two big patterned Japanese vases and a cloisonné jar of dried rose-leaves, under a picture of a lazy young shepherd, whom his flock were arousing from sleep. There were also a big sepia print of a painting of Napoleon in his youth, looking as pure and appealing as a poet, which was thought to resemble our Uncle Win, and—upstairs—old engravings of *The Journey of Life: Childhood, Youth, Manhood, Old Age*; and a pair of mythological pictures: one of Psyche descending into the underworld with the shaggy heads of Cerberus in the background, and the other of Pandora opening her box and releasing the shadowy spirits of Evil. Both maidens were as oval-faced and limpid-eyed as the girls in the illustrations for the collected poems of Thomas Bailey Aldrich. Both were quite undismayed, for their innocence was unassailable: Cerberus might well have been a neighbor's dog that barked rather badly at callers, and the fatal box a lamp that was smoking.

The dining-room, with its rack of blue plates and its straight chairs drawn up to the table, was a little more formal and serious; but it was interesting on account of its window-seats, which opened and in which we kept our toys, and on account of a large yellow jar, mottled with a pattern of daisies, which was always full of cookies. These cookies were rather rich, and each was studded in the middle with a raisin. The jar in which they were kept was like a symbol of our grandmother's life: dignified and decorative without, full of comfort for human appetites within. Our grandmother was always pleased to be thought to look like Queen Victoria.

On the other side of the hall from the living room was our grandfather's library and office. He had not, on account of his ill health, been able to practice much since they had moved into the new house at Laurelwood, and I hardly remember it before his death. Of the professional side of the room there is little now left in my picture except an acrid odor of medicine, a desk with a large wire wastebasket in which my cousin used to hunt for stamps, and a glass jar of sugar pills, which Grandfather used sometimes to let us eat. But at the opposite end of the longish room were the big terrestrial globe, the cribbage boxes, the backgammon board, the red and white ivory chessmen, and the bookcases, which reached almost to the ceiling and were ornamented by two small stuffed owls.

The foundation of this library was histories and the old Bohn translations of the classics. My grandfather used to say in his later years that he had been reading history all his life and that he was never again going to read anything but novels. The more I read history and the older I grow, the more I understand what he meant. But he had also many out-of-the-way books that appealed to his taste for the marvelous: the Finnish epic, the *Kalevala*, from which Longfellow had taken the meter for *Hiawatha*; a fascinating book on Russian folklore by that pioneer scholar William Ralston; several works of which all I can remember is that they contained rather terrifying pictures of prehistoric animals and oriental gods; and a treatise on the spirit world, with many authentic drawings of ghosts, which had been given him by a spiritualist friend in the North American Phalanx. My grandfather had much frequented this Fourierist community, one of the most successful and longest-lived of the Socialist experiments of the forties, which was not far from his former home; had listened to their social theories, looked at their paintings, read their verse. He was also on excellent terms with all the best local chess players, and he had bound files of the chess magazines, which always supplied him with problems. It was one of the great legends of the family that he had once beaten the turbaned automaton which played chess in the Eden Musée in New York and which was supposed to be mysteriously invincible; later on he had met a well-known champion, who had said to him: "Dr. Kimball, do you know that you beat me the other day?"

My grandfather's ideas on philosophy and religion were derived from Spencer and Mill, but he preferred those long, old-fashioned, formless books full of amusing or curious things, such as Burton's *Anatomy of Melancholy* and the *Noctes Ambrosianae*, which one does not so much follow through as drop in on from time to time, like the house of a learned friend. He loved Percy's *Reliques* and *The Ingoldsby Legends* and used to read them aloud to his children. He read them, also, the poetry of Scott, after whom he had been named Walter Scott by a mother infatuated with Waverley. He had also J. A. Symonds's

*Greek Poets,* which he had bought at second-hand and which, I was told, was one of the only extravagances in which he allowed himself to indulge at the time when he was cutting down on everything in order to send his children to good schools and colleges; and I was actually fed classical mythology as assiduously by my mother's family as I was instructed in the Scriptures by my father's. I remember that on one occasion at Laurelwood when I had been left alone with an uncle, a great sportsman and diner-out, who thought he ought to do something about me, his immediate and only idea was to lie on the sofa and read to me out of Bulfinch's *Age of Fable,* whose summaries I found rather dry after the *Tanglewood Tales* and Kingsley's *Greek Heroes.*

At the opposite corner of the house and opening out of the dining room was my grandmother's little conservatory, with its warm smell of flowers and earth. Below the long panes that let in the sunlight and on a shelf that ran around the room, there were boxes of raw dirt; and in the corners, lying or standing, were groups of red clay flower-pots telescoped into one another. Pricking up through the earth of the boxes and pots would be little lines of grasslike sproutings. I remember red geranium, purple heliotrope and pink hair-dangling bleeding-heart; and climbing up the strings against the windows were orange-and-yellow nasturtiums and morning-glories, purple, pink or blue. My grandmother was wonderful with flowers. "Everything grew for her," my mother says. From the first warmth of neutral days of March,

161

when white snowdrops and purple-veined crocuses were breaking the pale grass of the lawn, all the seeds and bulbs and plants and bushes seemed to come to life at her touch or from some silent understanding with her: white bridal-wreath, yellow forsythia, the delicate hennins of the columbine in purple and yellow and red, all the variety of peonies and tulips and roses that glowed and burned through the summer. And there were the things that did not make a brilliant show but which were cultivated for their charming odors: lemon verbena, mignonette, a big shrub-bush. We used to crush the shrubs to make them fragrant and carry them around in our pockets. We were made to feel that all these plants were precious. Some of them were family possessions, which had been brought down from upstate New York and which were passed along in slips to nieces and married daughters.

Thus the library at one corner of the house and the conservatory at the other had something of the sacredness of chambers which had been set aside by our grandparents for their cultivation, respectively, of intellectual and of aesthetic interests apart from their professional and family affairs, and in the case of my boy cousin and myself, the pursuits of literature and botany came to figure among our principal pastimes. Before we were able to write decently, we dictated several short novels to our, herself rather literary, aunt, who wrote them out in little paper books especially sewed together for the purpose. It was this aunt who taught us to study wild flowers and gave us books in which to look them up: *How to Know the Wild Flowers* and *Flowers and Ferns in Their Haunts.*

The hunt for these gave purpose to our walks —those long walks in the afternoons up and down the hilly streets of residences, where the trees were animated by squirrels and where downpours of acorns in autumn sprinkled the pavements and grass; or all the way around the lake through the pinewoods by paths of white sand and brown needles, which were lined with the pink coral pentagons of laurel or the low-growing wintergreen berries that were bright red and bit pulpy. I remember, too, the waxy pipsissewa and the livid-white Indian pipe which seemed so much the appropriate flowerings of those silent and monotonous woods. There were more exotic things in the swamps: an abundance of the fly-trapping pitcher plant, with its sensational scarlet flowers and its hair-lined and green-lipped gorges, which we carefully used to dig up with its boggy turf clinging about it, and keep in a bowl and watch. Our great hope was to find the scarcer orchids: arethusa and the yellow lady's-slipper. I remember my excitement and elation when I ran into a country boy selling white and yellow water-lilies and saw that he had among them a stalk or two of lady's-tresses, a white and exquisite tiny orchid. I bought them from him and then had qualms because I felt I ought to have found them myself.

## II

One of the great musical motifs of life at Laurelwood was the canter of horses' hoofs that came in to us from the wood-paved street. There was a riding academy almost opposite the house, and I have remembered out-of-door Laurelwood as a place where people were always on horseback or driving around in smart turnouts: men and boys in leather puttees, and girls with long skirts sitting side- saddle, in black riding habits and derbies; glossy victorias and carriages, with now and then a tallyho or a tandem. And there were also the polo games: the green field with its straight white lines, the headlong riders with their shirts ballooning, the mêlées of slender-legged horses, the low boards between us and the play, against which the furiously driven ball would woodenly bump and rebound. It was supposed to be a treat to watch polo, but I got rather a painful impression from the bloody flanks of the horses.

We had our fibres in this outside Laurelwood, but a good deal of it lay beyond us. It was both wealthier and gayer than we were. The more notorious scandals of the place were affairs that my mother and aunt used to hear of and laugh about, but which did not touch them closely. The story that came through to me most clearly involved an Episcopalian rector, who had been given a dig in *Town Topics* in connection with his supposed attentions to some widow or married lady. I think he threatened to sue the magazine.

Its editor, Colonel Mann, was later convicted of blackmail. The off-color publicity of *Town Topics* tainted all such places as Laurelwood in that period.

My uncle, who had read me Bulfinch, was a part of this outer world. He had brown eyes, round, bland and humorous, a handsome mustache in the style of Guy de Maupassant, and an attractive *blagueur* manner; his great retort was the baffling "You don't say!" He was always very smartly dressed and usually wore a flower in his buttonhole. He always carried his money in a roll and used to have bills of large denominations. He went to Europe every May and would invariably bring back for my mother and aunt a supply of silk stockings from Paris. He would produce them from the side pockets of his jacket and hand them over with an unconcern which elicited my admiration: his gaze was entirely devoid of the personal concentration of one who is bestowing a gift, and he never acknowledged the expressions of gratitude but would be talking about something else. He would hand me bright new dimes in the same way, usually after doing tricks with them. He used also to pass on to my mother and aunt a good many of the presents of jewelry which people seemed always to be giving him. Periodically he would turn up at my grandmother's with a lady—a Miss who had been "out" a long time or a Mrs. whose husband had vanished—whom he would present to his mother and sisters, in the same casual wide-eyed manner, as the woman he was going to marry. But none of these ladies lasted long: some of them appeared only once;

the next summer, after his trip to Europe, he would
arrive with a new fiancée. What I most liked to have
him do—though it was a part of his deadpan insou-
ciance not immediately to notice my requests—was
perform that old popular number, *The Man Who
Broke the Bank at Monte Carlo,* with his derby or
his straw hat tilted over one eye and his cane held
horizontal under his arm. He was also splendid with
*Sweet Marie.*

One day he took me to the house of some people
whom I shall call Finch, to play with a boy of about
my own age. My uncle drove me there in his light
little runabout. The Finches were not only far the
richest people in Laurelwood: they were among the
richest people in the world. Their house was hidden
away in a large estate surrounded by a high enclosure.
This enclosure was a thick black iron grille with a
murderous row of spikes along the top, and it had
roused in me the same kind of antagonism as the
rowelling of the polo horses. Mr. J. J. Finch was the
son of a great grabber and wrecker of railroads, one
of the contrivers of a market-cornering conspiracy
which had compromised a President of the United
States. When old Sam Finch had died, he had left to
the management of his son the greater part of a for-
tune of over a hundred million dollars. I did not, of
course, know at that time all that I now know about
the Finches—I did not know, for example, that old
Sam Finch had become before his death one of the
most generally hated men in America; but J. J. had
acquired for me some vaguely sinister value. He was

166

never around when I visited the house; but somebody pointed him out to me at the railroad station one morning, and I remember him as tall, lean and dark, with a short black mustache and an intent yet absent eye: the whole figure at once falconlike and detached.

There was, however, nothing in the least forbidding about Mrs. J. J. Finch, whom we found when we drove up before the big façade, standing at the top of the steps in a light dress and a wide summer hat, just putting on her gloves to go out. She looked much younger than one might have expected. I had heard that she had once been an actress, and I felt that her ready smile, her instinct to be nice and to be liked, as well perhaps as the sort of stage picture she made standing at the top of the steps, especially derived from this past. She sent for young Master James.

Young James was a black-haired little boy in socks and a sailor suit. I remember him as having heavy eyebrows, and he evidently resembled his father. At his mother's direction, he showed me through the house as if it were an historic building. As I had never then seen Fontainebleau or Versailles, it was the largest human residence that I had ever entered. I was struck by the fact that the furniture looked small in the immense rooms. Supplementing my memory at this point by a reference to Gustavus Myers, I find that this furniture was Louis XIV and that it was "blazing with powdered gold and covered with deep crimson velvet." This was the "great main

hall," which had also a "superb marble fireplace," a
hundred and fifty cut-glass pendants, a "massive
elliptical staircase of marble and bronze, supported
by marble columns," and a mural, which I remem-
ber, of the Canterbury pilgrims, sixteen feet high
and eighty feet long, which covered three sides of
the room.

I cannot pretend that I was not much impressed
by all this, but it was a palace rather without en-
chantment. I asked about James's toys and was es-
corted upstairs to the nursery. This tour, like every-
thing else, took place under the surveillance of a
governess, who never left us to ourselves for a mo-
ment. The toys were the largest I had ever seen ex-
cept as showpieces at Schwarz's in New York, and
it was hard for me to imagine playing with them.
James himself seemed rather indifferent to them ex-
cept in the case of such things as bats and rackets,
and his soldier and Indian outfits, which were actu-
ally complete suits of clothes instead of the usual
flimsy pretenses. They were hung up in a regular
wardrobe; and I felt a little abashed and resentful, as
if I were troubled at discovering that James had the
privilege of changing his role like an actor or a prince.
There was a rocking-horse that pulsated on springs
and a life-size woolly sheep, which belonged to
James's younger sister. This little girl presently ar-
rived and asserted a kind of sovereignty which was
also very unlike play.

The little girl's nurse was an oldish woman, who
spoke with a foreign accent—German I think it must

have been. It seemed to be part of her duties never to
stop talking—humorously and very rapidly, keeping
everybody under control—and somehow I did not like
her. In the conservatory—a great cage of glass, luxuri-
ant, humid and heavy with plant smells, so exotic, with
its parrots and palms, that it did not occur to me to
compare it with my grandmother's conservatory at
home—this staccato and glib woman seemed to me
particularly uncanny. I remember that she cautioned
James sharply against fooling with a certain gorgeous
red macaw, which sat, sullen and savage-looking,
chained by his leg to the perch, but that she paid a
great deal of attention to a very small and shabby
green parrot. She kept insisting, "He can whistle
*Yankee Doodle*"; but her wheedling, which went on
for some time, elicited nothing but croaked monosyl-
lables and wordless interrogations. It was a little as
if she were a witch conversing with a cherished
familiar; and the parrot himself showed some perver-
sity, for after she had given it up and we had turned
our backs to go out, we heard a soft faltering piping
behind us; it was indeed *Yankee Doodle*, broken up
queerly and perfectly expressionless.

Outside, when we got to the stables, young James
showed a little more interest. He had a miniature
automobile, which his father had had specially built
for him and which was a newspaper wonder at that
period when automobiles of any kind were rare. I
learn from Myers that there were also "a great tan-
bark hippodrome, a gymnasium, bowling alleys and
lounging rooms, a shooting gallery, a large swimming

pool and Turkish and Russian baths"; but I don't remember seeing all these. What I do remember distinctly is a theater. I assumed as a matter of course, when it was shown me, that it was used for amateur theatricals, but was informed by young James that his father had regular musical comedy companies come down from New York and give shows in it. I imagined an elegant audience, in diamonds, white shirt-fronts and tails, watching *Fantana* or *The Prince of Pilsen.*

The walks were carefully gravelled and they were decorated with marble statues. These statues seemed so remote from the classical gods and goddesses whom I had come to know through Kingsley and Hawthorne and whom they must have been supposed to represent that I did not even try to identify them. There was a sunken Italian garden—the estate was called Florentine Court—which I suggested might be a good place to play in, but it was made clear to me that this was out of the question. I was amazed and somewhat embarrassed to observe that there was a man standing by with a rake, whose role was to smooth the gravel when anyone had walked or driven over it.

We amused ourselves—on this and on subsequent visits—in ways that rather bored me. My new friend was not nearly so entertaining as my cousin. He was a perfectly good-natured boy with neither humor nor imagination. Though he cared nothing about books or botany, he had learned something about the various sports, and we used to have jumping matches

and play catch and knock out flies—contests in which
I was usually defeated. One afternoon when it had
been raining, we sailed things on a big puddle in the
lawn, while the governess—James's English governess
—sat on a marble bench and kept telling him not to
get his clothes dirty. James, however, had got hold of
a large log, which he wanted me to help him drag to
the water. I objected that the log would not float
because it was too big and heavy. James declared that
it would. A considerable argument ensued, in which
I upheld my position dogmatically and with absolute
assurance. I was abashed when we at last launched
the log in the puddle and it turned out that it did
perfectly float. I found that I was piqued by the fact
that this son of a millionaire, who seemed to me
totally uneducated, should have a grasp of this pri-
mary phenomenon of physics as to which I had so
flatly blundered.

But the incident of my visits to the Finches' which
most struck me and remained with me most vividly
happened one afternoon when we were driving
around the place in a pony-cart that belonged to
James's sister. (I had been surprised to discover how
very little the Finch children knew about Laurel-
wood: they were not often allowed to see other chil-
dren or to go anywhere outside their own domain.)
James, who was driving, had stopped the cart and
had ordered the footman—they had a footman even
for the pony-cart—to get out and bring him some
apples which he had seen under a tree in a field. The
governess remonstrated with him: "They're too green.

They'll make you ill"; but James said he wanted the apples. The governess called him "James, dear," and, apparently lacking the authority to command, she began to try to persuade him: the argument lasted several minutes. Then James repeated his order: "Get out and get them," he said to the man, who had sat without moving—"you should have done it when I told you the first time." The man got down and went for the apples. It was not that the boy was perverse or that he had wanted to be disagreeable with his governess: he sometimes called her "darling" in a reversion to some childish emotion which embarrassed me by something like passion, as if she had taken the place of his mother, and his tone here had not been petulant. But he was firm that it should be understood that he was issuing the orders, not taking them, and that people were to jump at his bidding. For when the footman had gone after the apples, he turned to the governess and said: "These men must do their duty, Anna!"

The words long rang in my mind. I was shocked by them and did not like them. I should never have been allowed to behave like that, and it would never have occurred to me to speak like that to or about a servant. The incident dropped a partition between the Finches and me.

### III

I first wrote down the memories above in the winter and spring of 1918 at the table of a café in northern

France. It is queer to be working on something from a manuscript of more than twenty years ago, written in an immature hand quite different from my present one and on pages of gray paper ruled crisscross, the only kind I had been able to buy at the *mercerie* in that little wartime town in the Vosges. It brings back the cold mists, the bad French stoves, the nights with everything darkened on account of German planes, the eating of hot soup through smothering colds. That was the winter the French Army mutinied. It is strange to reflect that all that is already longer ago than those incidents at Laurelwood were at the time I first tried to describe them.

And why *should* I have tried to describe them in 1917-18, when there was obviously so much else to think about? And why, more than twenty years later, should I go back to them again today? What I got out of them, when I first put them down, was a contrast, which I made rather smugly, between the old American society and the new. Today I know a number of things which I did not know, or did not understand, then. To be sure, what has happened to the Finch family has justified any assumptions that I might at that time have been entertaining as to the basic unsoundness of millionaire princes. Old man Finch, the son of a poor farmer, had worked assiduously at his financial villainy and had had no appetite for social exploits. But his son liked to give immense parties and to shine in foreign lands; he assumed that the special genius for capturing and controlling railroads was transmissible through heredity; he neglected those tiresome trips to the West that were essential for checking up on his properties; and he ultimately fell a victim to a rival capitalistic brontosaurus who had just hatched out of the swamp and was still in the aggressive phase. The other members of the family, alarmed, had him removed as trustee of the estate, which was rapidly crumbling away. Some of the women supplied classical examples of the type of American heiress whose family buys her a title. I think the little girl I saw was one of them. My friend James eloped several years ago with a girl from a New Jersey drug-store not far from his old home in Laurelwood. Their palace itself was disposed of to a Catholic college for girls some fifteen years ago.

Yet, after all, I am well aware today that our own family had been drawn into the orbit of the power represented by the Finches. The special sort of felicity we enjoyed in going to my grandmother's house was due to a peculiar peace and ease which depended on my grandmother's self-confidence. In our own homes—both my cousins' and mine—we had felt, without knowing it, the tension of the times. Neither their father nor mine was the kind of man who thrived in a period of that sort. Both had had the old professional education, and the effort to maintain a position in the society after the Civil War, when all the forces of exploitation had cut loose and nothing as yet had been done to curb them, was a strain on the old-fashioned American. One had either to overwork, as my uncle did, in order to keep up with the new standard of living; or if, as my father did, one refused to keep up beyond a certain point and went on acting on a set of principles at a tangent from the accepted ones, to incur a certain isolation. But I was surprised to learn later from my father that the Laurelwood house itself had been a product of the impulse to keep up. Another odor which I vividly remember from it is the smell of fresh reservoir water running out of nickel-plated faucets into the kind of white-enamelled bath and basin which in our own home we had not yet had installed to take the place of the old wood-and-tin kind. My grandfather had come gradually to abandon his country practice of the farms and small towns for richer patients on the Jersey coast; my grandmother had wanted to live at Laurelwood and she had wanted the beautiful modern new house. My grandfather still had his rich patients there, because that was where they went in winter; but the expense of building the house had put a tax on his later years, when his health was seriously failing and when he would certainly have been content, so far as he himself was concerned, to spend his remaining time with his friends and his books and his chess. Had I not myself, at home in Red Bank, a certain arrogance of the spoiled only child, who is safe and unassailable in his own home domain? May there not have been some spirit of competition in the resentment I felt toward the Finch boy?

My uncle, who took me to the Finches, went on with my grandfather's practice; but, after his early days of promise as a surgeon, he turned into a fashionable doctor who came to spend more and more of his time on the yachts and at the bridge-tables of the rich. In his fifties he was drinking pretty heavily and suffering from terrible depressions. When I later read my grandmother's diary, I saw that he was her favorite son, and it was suggested to me by someone in the family that his intimate relation with her had been the reason for his never marrying. One day, at the time when my cousins and I were growing up and going to prep school, our uncle had us come to lunch with him in Laurelwood. He announced with his bland unconcern, which had impressed me so much as a child, that he was going to die very soon and that he had arranged to leave his library to me and his watch and his gun to my cousin. We were shocked and did not know what to say. I felt that the fine eyes that looked beyond us were now really quite indifferent to the effect which he was producing on others. He did die very soon, of apoplexy, all alone at night, in his apartment in one of the Laurelwood hotels, which was the only home he had ever had in that place of magnificent residences. His books consisted partly of those elaborate sets—*Secret Court Memoirs of Europe* and so forth—which used to be brought out in costly bindings and sold to people like the Finches, and which people like the Finches had given him; but they included also other things: Kipling, Stevenson, Balzac, the eighteenth-century novelists—which were not only well bound but worth having.

I know now that the tides of society can give a new configuration to all but the strongest personalities, if they do not sweep them away. Yet I have dug out again these memories, trifling enough in themselves, in order to make again the contrast between my grandfather's house and the Finches'; and on reflection I have come to the conclusion that I am impelled to recur to these incidents under a stress, at first largely unconscious, of being frightened about the things I have a stake in. It was so at the time of the first World War, and it is so again today. For that ride in the Finches' pony-cart was the moment when it was definitely revealed to me that there were other kinds of people in the world who did not think and behave like my own family and who were yet at the same time important—that they might be even more important than we were; and the first time I remember to have asserted to myself the superior virtue and value of certain things which had reached me through my grandparents—of the spirit that studies and understands against the spirit that acquires and consumes; of the instinct to give light and life against the lethal concentration on power; of the impulse that acts to minimize the social differences between human beings instead of trying to keep them up and make them wider; and of the kind of ambition that attempts to build on this thought and creative instinct and fellowship instead of on the authority of the pony-cart.

THREE RELIQUES

OF

ANCIENT WESTERN POETRY

COLLECTED FROM THE RUINS

OF THE TWENTIETH CENTURY

1951

# The Mass in the Parking Lot

. . . And whom should we meet there, on the loose,
But André Gide in a big burnoose.
What were his words of wisdom? Damn it,
He was whooping it up for Dashiell Hammett.
More correctly garbed, we encountered later
T. S. Eliot, the Great Dictator.
Having just awakened from troubled sleep,
He told us Charles Williams was terribly deep.
And Wystan Auden, with rigorous views
But his necktie hanging around his shoes,
Expounded his taste for detective stories,
Which he reads to illumine the current mores.
But all—with the single exception of Gide,
Who prefers sailor Melville's more masculine breed—
Were exceedingly strong for Henry James,
With his stunningly high artistic aims.
"I've made a discovery! Isn't it thrilling?
He's as good as Stendhal," cried Lionel Trilling.
With a rumble-de-bum and a pifka-pafka
Came the fife-and-drum corps parading for Kafka.
Full of multiple meanings and *sotto voce's*,
They had more and more grown to resemble roaches:
Thus debasing themselves, they drew close to the
    Master,
And could crawl into cracks to avoid disaster.

The scene was a desolate parking lot,
In an undetermined suburban spot,
Though few of us had any cars to park,
And the air was bad and the day was dark.
And most were agreed they must hold a mass
To bring some poignant epiphka to pass;
But the problem was who should officiate,
Who lead the choir, who pass the plate.
Roman Catholics, cheek by jaw,
Sat Graham Greene and Evelyn Waugh;
But Waugh, with his wiles and his wicked jokes,
Was keen to bring in the county folks,
While Graham, a child of the Scots and the Picts,
Liked the richer and riper derelicts.
Eliot and Auden, Anglo-Caths,
Amateur clergymen, lean as laths,
Morally snobbish but madly self-humbling,
Made an almost inaudible mumbling bumbling.
And Huxley was brewing a new brand of Yogi
To banish the bestial sexual bogey,
While Isherwood, lately a Quaker nudist,
Had turned Anglo-American Babist-Buddhist.
And that gentleman-caterer Somerset Maugham,
Whom they amiably praised since he couldn't awe
        'em,
The prince of chain-restaurant pastry-cooks,
Had been dashing a flavor of God in his books
—Though what flavor it was I shall never know,
For I cannot get down his unleavened dough.
So they argued with moderate animation
And well-planted accents of abnegation,

Till somebody said, "It won't be so hard
If we all concentrate on Kierkegaard."

And they fixed up a flimsy receiving set,
Over which, with some fussing, they managed to
        get—
Through a cracked screech of Marxism, still fanatic,
And a rattle of Existentialist static—
A Voice that said, "Fellows, I've got a new sponsor.
If you're sending Me prayers and you want an answer.
Turn to Alpha Omega XYZ
At nine-thirty tonight for a load of Me.
You've already discovered the wonderful fun it
Affords to find God in a dim who-dun-it—
How *The Trial, The Castle, The Ambassadors*
Ooze purest religion from all their pores.
Well, boys, you must see Me on television,
Where I wallop my points with appalling precision.
I'm the brains of a flickering comic-strip
That lets all the most hideous instincts rip.
On the one hand, the treacherous heretics
Are implacably conked with brutal bricks;
While the saint is popped off, an exploded zero—
Though to you boys, perhaps, an inferior hero.
It's only the sinner with faith who wins,
For he's saved by his faith, and you're thrilled by his
        sins:
He's a beautiful bum who always escapes,
Just gasping a prayer when perdition gapes.
You may find this a little bit crude—but I doubt it:
I believe that you boys will be mad about it!"

183

And I watched it begin—a wavering splotch
Made a big comic rabbit—I had to watch,
In a clamp of compulsion I couldn't shake,
Till, choking and groaning, I burst awake.
The lights were on and the windows closed,
Just as they had been when I dozed;
And below me lay flaccidly sprawling near
An avant-garde quarterly (well in the rear)
That had slumped to the floor with unheeded flop
When my slackening fingers had let it drop.

# Reversals, or *Plus ça change*\*

The man in the tavern was livid
And told him to go to the Devil:
    "Your appearance is sneaking and snide—
    At my table no vagabond dines!
Your walk has the slink of a felon
Whose alphabet starts with an aleph.
    Be off with your blustered appeals—
    In my blankets you never shall sleep!"
Said the stranger: "I flee from the tsar of
This blind and Siberian forest.
    You hate him, too: help me to hide—
    For else I shall certainly die.
I have ridden for days without stirrups,
Misled by invisible spirits,
    Not daring to stop at a town
    In dread of the noose or the knout.
I have gnawed at the birch-trees, the nude ones,
Have slept in the lee of the snow-dune;
    I have shuddered awake with a sigh
    When the branches were dropping their ice.
I have skirted the Arctic ice-cap-floe,
Escaped from the fangs of the wolf-pack—
    Less fierce than the claws of that brute
    Whose impudence none can perturb!—

\* This backward-rhyming meter, known as amphisbaenics, which is often found in late twentieth century poetry, is a characteristic product of that baffled and ambiguous period.

185

That monster whose mere nod annihilates
Millions!"—"Good God, you are Stalin, a
    Fugitive! What a mean face
    Without whiskers! Must I keep you safe
In my lonely old inn on the border
I have had more than one horrid Red rob?
    Begone!" He banged-to the door—
    Then opened—in accents less rude:
"Well, so be it, enemy comrade:
Both exiles and outcasts, we dare mock
    These powers that last for a day,
    Till a nightfall when nothing can aid.
Come in: such occasions are rare if
One dwells in the wilds. I was Führer!"
    The Russian dashed in with a shriek
    And swallowed a bottle of kirsch.
"Be at ease: we shall gossip, shall *review*.
Who is this new tsar, say." "One Hoover—
    An old pro-consul of theirs.
    My mustaches make bays for his wreath."

# Cardinal Merry Del Val

## I

Now, Cardinal Merry del Val
   Had just had a cognac with Pope Pius—
He was humming a gay madrigal
   As he came down the stairs on the bias.
As he passed by the Vatican guard
   In their peppermint tights and striped breeches,
He would now and then drop a droll word
   That had all the big fellows in stitches.
"You know me, lads—never a prude!
I was once a good friend of Pirelli."
   And he gave a broad wink
   That turned some of them pink.
"But long live our leader, Pacelli!"

For Cardinal Merry del Val
   Was, oh, what a wonderful pal!
They laughed ha ha ha and they laughed hee hee
     hee!
The sweetest old prelate that ever you see
   Was Cardinal Merry del Val.

*"Ay ay ay ay!*
*Canta y no llores,*
*Porque cantando se alegran . . ."*
   Sang Cardinal Merry del Val.

"Remember, lads, never be shy
  Nor patronize rubber or padlock—
Be eager, be lusty, be spry!—
  That is, if you do it in wedlock.
Never leave your fair bride in the lurch
  If you would not incur our reproaches.
You'll be making more souls for the Church
  If you're breeding like rats and like roaches.
If a Catholic stoops to control,
May his condom contain a Houdini!"
  And he made a bold thrust
  At the bountiful bust
Of a beautiful bronze by Bernini.

  "Oh, life is a bright carnival
  For a Catholic boy or a gal.
They laugh ha ha ha and they laugh ho ho ho,
And they shall have kiddies wherever they go!"
  Said Cardinal Merry del Val.

*"Oi Mari, oi Mari,*
*Quanta suonne aggio perso per te!*
*Fammi dormi . . ."*
  Sang Cardinal Merry del Val.

## III

"Ah, the Catholic Church loves the poor—
  The more people are helpless the better.

188

For poverty Christ has no cure,
    Yet the Vatican's never a debtor.
If at home you're a bit down at heels,
    If your children don't flourish or fatten,
You can always make sure of your meals
    By hopping a boat to Manhattan.
Yes, go to the great U.S.A.,
Where you'll have the fine chance to improve yez,
    Where we breed the big crooks
    And we ban the bad books
And there's nothing but Catholic movies.


    "Yes, sail to the home of Saint Al,
    A dandy American pal,
Where we're training at Fordham and at Holy Cross
The Pope, the Black Pope and the Tammany Boss,"
    Said Cardinal Merry del Val.


*"And it's all day long they say, 'I—love—you!'*
*Sure the boys are all mad about Nelly,*
*The daughter of Officer Kelly . . ."*
    Sang Cardinal Merry del Val.


#### IV

"And literature!—boys, it's a boom,
    With our Maritains, D'Arcys and Sheens—
It's a wholesale stampede to the womb
    Such as hasn't been witnessed in aeons!
They come to us, weary and weak,
    No matter how mad or how modern:

I believe we shall very soon speak
    Of Spellman—not Spender—and Auden.
What desperate fools they look now—
Your Dos Passoses, Malrauxs and Koestlers!"
    And he made a swift pass
    At the well-polished ass
Of one of Praxiteles' wrestlers.


    "When you've glimpsed the abyss of Pascal,
    You will need a reliable pal.
You will have a bad head when your Marxism fails,
And you cannot do better than snatch at Christ's
        nails!"
    Said Cardinal Merry del Val.


*"April is the cruelest month,*
*So let's give a rouse for King Charles,*
*And Saint Charles Baudelaire's Fioretti du Mal,"*
    Chanted Cardinal Merry del Val.


v

"You may talk of your Soviet State,
    With its clever police and its purges:
A power that throttles debate
    And procures recantation with scourges.
We had all of that ages ago—
    We're adept at such work, we adore it.
If that's what the world wants, let us know:
    We'll be only too glad to restore it!
How much simpler a single strong Church

Than this welter of secular movements!
    What a lark to get back
    To the screw and the rack
And to give them some modern improvements!

    "If that's what you call rad*ical*,
    We'll bring you a red baccha*nal*—
If that's your conception of freeing the masses,
We're better than Lenin, my lads and my lasses!"
    Cried Cardinal Merry del Val.

*"C'est la lutte finale!*
*Groupons-nous, car demain*
*L'Internationale sera du genre humain* . . .
And *we'll* be your Internationale!"
    Added Cardinal Merry del Val.

# A CHRISTMAS STOCKING

## FUN FOR YOUNG AND OLD

### 1953

# Scurrilous Clerihews

## THE PARADOX OF THORNTON WILDER

Thornton Wilder
Couldn't be milder;
And yet, by gracious,
He's rather erinaceous!

———

## ENEMIES OF PROMISE

Cyril Connolly
Behaves rather fonnily:
Whether folks are at peace or fighting,
He complains that it keeps him from writing.

———

## THE ART OF EDUCATION

Gilbert Highet
Cried, "Lux fiat!"
Though the skies remained dark,
It was rather a lark.

John Dos Passos
No longer writes for the Masses,
And when he returns to his Virginia estate, he
   is greeted by a chorus of "Old Massa!" 's.
On account of Soviet knavery,
He favors restoring slavery.

## e. e. cummings, esquirrel

In your Greenwich Village slummings,
You may still find e. e. cummings
Residing at 4 Patchin Place
And writing his name lower case:
A fixed point of effervescence,
With a touch of deliquescence.

## THE TATES

Allen Tate
Is slightly out of date—
As is his devoted mate,
Caroline Gordon Tate.

---

Andy and Katharine White
Are never completely right,
Yet preserve in a remarkable manner
In corpore non sano mens sana.

---

THE WALKERS

Charlie Walker
Is an indefatigable talker.

Adelaide Walker
Is an indefatigable talker.

---

METTERNICH'S GREAT ADMIRER

Clever Peter Viereck'll
Seem a bit more of a miracle
If he'll hold himself in a particle
And refrain from sending us offprints of his
        every godblessed article.

# Anagrams on Eminent Authors

A! TIS SOME STALE THORN.

———

{ I ACHE RICH BALLADS, M!
  A LIMBIR SCACH LAD HE!

———

I'M STAGY WHEN NEER.

———

LIVE MERMAN: HELL.

———

AWFUL KILLIN', ERMA!

———

MAKZ 'N NICE COMPOTE.

———

U DON PRAZE
E.P.—U ADORZ 'N'
PORZ, "A NU ED
P. EZ AROUND!"
U DON RAZ E.P.:
"UROP ENDZ A
PERZON. ADU,

OUR NAZE D.P.!
DAZER UPON
AZURE POND,
A NUD POZER
AND PURE OZ."

U REZPOND, "A
PROUD ZANE
UPROZE AND
RANUD 'OPEZ,
PORED NUZ, A-
ROUZD A PEN
RAZU, OPEND
DORZ UPAN E-
UROP. 'AZN'D 'E
URNED A PO'Z
PRAZE?" U NOD.

# Relaxed Crossword Puzzles

*(Solid squares of five-letter words, reading
across and down.)*

## I

My *first* is a garment that fastens behind;
  My *second* applies to a lush little lake;
My *third* in your *Handwörterbuch* you will find
  May mean whilst or because; my *fourth* is a fake:
The Association of Impotent Old Apoplectic Parties;
  My *fifth* is the steamship *Nigerian Royal Highness*;
My *sixth* a confection of musical art is;
  My *seventh* an organ remote from the sinus;
My *eighth* is a painter fantastic and French;
My *ninth* is exclaimed at a wrench or a stench;
And my *tenth* is a nimble but mythical wench.

## II

My *first* is whatever is fed to a mill;
  My *second* are passions that fiercely have racked us;
My *third* is a harbor of Rome, not a hill;
  My *fourth* is a perfume contrived to attract us;
My *fifth* stands for sovereigns retired in Russia;
  My *sixth* we may do in indulging my second;
My *seventh* is what must befall human treasure;
  My *eighth* a great goddess by Babylon reckoned,

200

Misspelled by a scribe in a very bad text;
  By my *ninth* we may climb—here a little misset
By a printer whose spirit was weary and vexed;
  The regime of my *tenth* we may sometimes regret.

# Easy Exercises in the Use of Difficult Words

## SEPTEMBER LANDSCAPE

The weather still continues hot,
Though autumn lanes lie filemot;
The sky, though scudding clouds now blotch it,
Wears April's tint, a tender watchet.

---

## NURSERY VIGNETTE

The bubbled baby gave an abrupt burp,
Her tiny face contorted in an irpe
(The *i* pronounced, perhaps, like *beard* not bird).
Ben Jonson only used this pleasant little word.

---

## PETER FLORESCENT, PETER MARCESCENT; PETER DEHISCENT, PETER RESIPISCENT

Having bloomed while dining out,
Peter, faded, craves a drop;
Peter, grounded with the gout,
Heaves a groan and hopes to stop.

---

## SCÈNE DE BOUDOIR

Said Philip Sidney, buttoning his jerkin,
"Allow me, darling: you have dropped your merkin."

---

## LAKESIDE

An old cob swan his cygnets thus addressed:
"Stray not too far from the parental nest.
Remember you can never be as spry as is
Yon falcon with her eyrie full of eyases!"

---

## HERALDIC BATTLE

I would not stake a battered copper stiver'n
The chances of your talbot with my wyvern!
The dragon, segreant, awaits the attack;
The dog, well guled, will gasp upon his back.

---

## PALACE DUSK

Byzantium broods some horrid deed tonight,
Where catamawfreys clot the dying light.

—This queer and mystifying word, I see,
Is not included in the O. E. D.
Will someone well-versed in the Byzantines
Explain to me precisely what it means?

# Brief Comments on Mistaken Meanings

## JUNK

We have done admirably, I confess,
To scrap that dreadful word *anotherguess*.
In Fielding it still lurks to inspire terror
Or make us think we've struck a printer's error.
Browning revived it, as he would, of course;
But we may let it lie without remorse.

———

## A DREAM FOR DANIEL UPDIKE

It may be, reader, that you do not care if
You cannot tell a *seraph* from a *serif*,
But serifs and sans-serifs singing see
Around the Throne in endless ecstasy.

———

## WORDS ACROSS THE CHANNEL

*Piepowder, Rotten Row,* and *kickshaw*—those
Are *Route du roi, pied poudreux, quelque chose.*
The English always give a nasty wrench
To anything they're forced to take from French.

*Bifteck, bouledogue, milord, jazz-hot, higlif*—
To these one passes with distinct relief;

By such, one is less horrified than charmed:
Though nicely trimmed, they are not quite deformed.

———

## LE BLUFF

Victor Hugo, that big but brilliant fake,
Imagined that an English *wapentake*
Was like a wyvern or a firedrake.
He never would acknowledge his mistake.

———

## THE PURIST'S COMPLAINT

*Jejune, transpire, ilk, demean*
Don't mean what you may think they mean—
  Nor *viable,*
  Nor *friable,*
Do look them up, old bean.
And do take pity, if it's not too late,
On *titivate* confused with *titillate.*

—And yet, it's undeniable
These meanings that are gross mistakes
Are creeping in the lexicons
Beside the old authentic ones,
Which may fade out beside the fakes.
  And this, I am afraid,
Is how the languages are made.

# Memories of the Poetry of the Nineties, Written Down While Waiting for Long-Distance Calls

## SONNET

*He dreams of cheese that never feared a mouse—*
　　So mocked our poet of an elder day;
　　And we who, idly dulcet, still essay
The palinode of these our *heres* and *nows*,
Whose palsied pulse may never more arouse
　　The mounting sap that swells the buds of May—
　　We scarce can tell the glimmer from the gray,
Nor, languid, loot September's laden boughs.

Ah, golden handmaids of Eurydice!
　　Wild woodland satyrs at their wanton sport!
Great Homer's comrades!—I would rather be
　　A beggar skulking the Piræan port
In sordid tatters, so I might but see
　　Old lusty Triton rising with a snort!

## DRAFTS FOR A QUATRAIN

The wind of dawning riffles the young furze;

Night { narrows to a solitary star;
wakes and wanly shudders, having slept;
veils a vigil sacred yet obscene;
muffles moonlight where the sands are
   dank;
glitters where the banquet lanterns
   glowed;

By { placid depths mysteriously stirs
haunted
troubled
teeming
turbid

{ The noon-expanding nenuphar.
The moon-ensorcelled nympholept.
The Proust-anointed neurasthene.
The snailly-gliding nudibranch.
The guest-eructed nesselrode.

# Miniature Dialogues

Said Mario Praz to Mario Pei,
"Che cosa noiosa the Great White Way!"
"But full of delightful polyglots!"
Said Mario Pei to Mario Praz.

———

Said Gayelord Hauser to Gathorne-Hardy,
"Aren't you getting a little lardy?"
"My nature's essentially that of a browser,"
Said Gathorne-Hardy to Gayelord Hauser.

———

COLLOQUY BETWEEN ONEIDA AND
LEWIS COUNTIES, NEW YORK

Said Walter Edmonds to Edmund Wilson,
"What river you say that old grist mill's on?"
"Some day you must show me your Indian dead
mounds,"
Said Edmund Wilson to Walter Edmonds.

# Something for my Russian Friends

## LE VIOLON D'INGRES DE SIRINE

Our perverse old писатель Vladimir
Was stroking a butterfly's femur.
  "I prefer this," he said,
  "To a lady in bed,
Or even a velvet-eyed lemur."

———

## FUN IN THE BALKANS

An intrepid young girl in Rumania
Enjoyed a unique ощущение
  When her boy-friend De Couille
  's extensible —
Transplanted her clear to Albania.

———

## AN INCIDENT OF THE OCCUPATION

Sacher-Masoch, that Austrian botch,
When a Red soldier asked for his watch,
  Said in faltering Russian
  And girlishly blushin',
"молодец, ты — мою мать!"

# Something for my Jewish Friends

ישעיה ברלין
Having made himself thin,
Said, „עתה מה אעשה?"
אמלך על ישראל?
או אשמר את כל-הנפשות?
Or both?
או אשא לאשה את היפה מכל הנערות בלנודוז?
מה אעשה אני?
All three?
Or none?"

# Something about the Author

There was an old werewolf named Wilson
Whose jaws were as strong as a Stillson;
   But when wanted one day
   To go after his prey,
They found he was sleeping off Pilsen.

✻

A message you'll expect, my friends,
Before our Christmas frolic ends.

—I write these lines in Talcottville,
My base of operations still:

Broad upstate pastures, Holstein cows;
And my old Lewis County house,

Gray-walled with Sugar River stone;
This room in which I sit alone,

With books and tables, all one asks,
Rotating interesting tasks,

In silences that hardly jog
A humming truck, a jangled dog.

—At dawn, on windows facing East,
A tree shows silhouette in mist;

Then, mounting, brimming from behind
That night-wet world, the skies unblind

A dazzling blazing flood of light
That drenches elms and drowns them white;

Then, brilliantly imbuing all,
Makes blue-green panels on my wall:

Far woods and alder-fringe that follow
Our little river live if shallow,
A field ploughed brown or clover-yellow;

Yet, opening a great world, reveals
The dim blue Adirondack hills.

—At evening, the green slopes are gold;
The August afternoon turns cold;

The high day ebbs—fluid and bright,
White, yellow, orange; blackest night

Blots all, obliterates the town;
Dark hills and woodlands, crowding down,

Confine us to the fortlike house;
We read abed; a lone cow lows.

A century and a half ago,
When all was wilderness and snow,

When women shivered, cattle died,
"Priest" Kimball brought his Mather bride

And preached hell-fire from Leyden Hill—
The corn, it's said, can't freeze there still.

But migrants from New England hills
Had hoped to leave, with other ills,

That menace of the Mather creed:
They found a man of milder breed

And gave my ancestor the sack;
Yet later had to have him back.

—The Talcotts, Tories at that date,
Resided here in feudal state.

They took a stiff old-fashioned stand,
Would not let artisans buy land—

Which progress-minded folks deplored;
Bought canvases and busts abroad.

—Another role was Thomas Baker's,
Who broke and sold the Talcott acres.

A profit-making Man of Ross,
He built the town, became its boss,

And in the legislature sat,
A rude Jacksonian Democrat.

—The Talcotts and the Bakers feuded:
Brought lawsuits, long resentments brooded,

Never to speak swore bitter vows;
The Talcotts claimed this Talcott house,

In which the Bakers now resided;
The countryside was all divided—

Yet gradually all subsided.

Unyielding still in principle,
They'd known each other long and well;

Already merged with one another,
Since Baker girl wed Talcott brother:

Both veterans of the Northern night,
Both nurselings of the Eastern light,
They found it profitless to fight.

—Two Kimballs paired with girls from each,
Who, worldlings, helped them not to preach.

Eventually they threw over
That brimstone-breathing black Jehovah;

Read Huxley, Hume and Mill, and then
They never went to church again.


Of these three strains the recent child,
I like to think them reconciled

In this old shell of stone that stands
As blocked and beamed by Talcott hands;

To pore at ease upon that past
And feel them all relaxed at last.

—So these the precepts are, my friends,
The aging Wilson recommends:

Beware of dogmas backed by faith;
Steer clear of conflicts to the death;

Keep going; never stoop; sit tight;
Read something luminous at night.

And if no ready means you find
To cultivate this state of mind,

Why, you must come to see me here
—If not next year, another year.

A CHRISTMAS DELIRIUM

1955

# The Children's Hour

And would you like to know, my dears,
How Father feels at sixty years,
And what he thinks? Then, gather round.
However doddering I sound,
However grumblingly I grope,
I'll leave you on a note of hope,
Illuming life from several angles,
To steer you through its twists and tangles.

Well, first you see, I'm growing stout:
I pant, and suffer pangs of gout—
Which people, when I limp and croak,
Are pleased to think a charming joke—
Not guessing how a gouty crisis
Makes even bedclothes squeeze like vises;
How casual knocks feel fiercely rude;
How constant pain must be subdued
By stiffish drinks, when dining out,
Which then result in further gout.
A remedy exists, of course,
But this seems sometimes almost worse
In ways of which I'll not discourse.
There's something new that one can get,
But this I haven't tested yet.

You've heard me quietly complain
At moments of another pain,

Which means, I hope, no vital harm,
But cramps the play of my right arm
And makes it difficult to swim.
Now, any twinge in any limb
Is called "bursitis" nowadays—
That is what every doctor says.
I wonder if it's not a word
That leaves unfathomed problems blurred,
Like "virus," "allergy" and "fungus."
I don't believe they know what's stung us.

You will, I think, be glad to hear
Those curious pricklings in my ear
That also prickled through my cheek,
Of which you've sometimes heard me speak
—And somewhat anxiously I spoke—
Do not presage an early stroke,
Which I've done little to deserve:
Mere twitchings of a facial nerve—
No worse than my right eyelid here
That twitched so constantly last year.

And then, the dimming of the senses:
I cannot eat without my lenses—
For theaters, another pair;
My hearing, I must say, is fair.
I often fall asleep by day,
But nights it's just the other way:
I rarely sleep without a pill,
And nightmares not by Freud but Brill.

—Enough of this! My serious points
Are not, of course, my crippled joints;
But, first, the halt and hobbled pace
One's elder self is forced to face:
When monster projects loom and lure,
When powers seem at last mature,
The wretched old physique decays.
One smoulders in a slump for days;
Goes blank on names; gaga, forgets
What one was saying; loses bets.
And yet the effort must be made,
The bell to take the stage obeyed,
The fire revived—
                              But I'm alone!
My audience, one by one, have gone;
Discouraged by my dreary squawk,
They've skipped the inspiration talk,
And left me to my Chinese checkers,
My mounds of books and Mozart Deccas,
For livelier games and lovely dates;
With urgent honks, they're hunting mates.

Ah, well, no matter—let them go!
My pressure has been ebbing low—
I'm not sure I could do it justice.
Besides, the young can never trust us.
Better, perhaps, I might compile,
From odds and ends I've kept on file,
A medley where a few old friends may find
What's really going on in Father's mind.

※

—What gaiety!

—Have you not heard? Mankind may be destroyed.

—Totally?

—Without exception.

*From the Geckese*

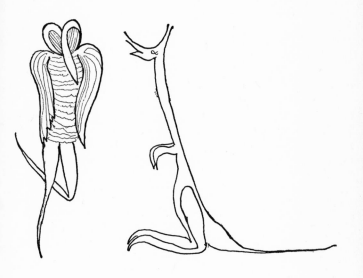

—Guess who!

—Tsk tsk—must you use scent?

*From the Geckese*

# Imaginary Dialogues

### "WITHIN THE RIM"

Said Lieutenant Henry to Henry James,
"They tell me you're not very hot with the dames."
"There are voids of the vulgar, my excellent
    Henry!". . .
Said Henry James to Lieutenant Henry.

### TWO NEW ENGLAND GIRLS

Said Louise Bogan to Phyllis Duganne,
"Sometimes I've thought I could dance with a fan."
"Stick close to the home is my present slogan,"
Said Phyllis Duganne to Louise Bogan.

### PETERHOF

Said Peter the Great to a Great Dane,
"Some people think I'm a little insane."
"I thought it was just that you growled when you
    ate,"
Said the Great Dane to Peter the Great.

### AT THE ALGONQUIN

Said Eustace Tilley to Tilly Losch,
"Will you join me, my dear, in a bout of squash?"
"You're very friendly, but don't be silly,"
Said Tilly Losch to Eustace Tilley.

### A GHOST OF OLD BALTIMORE

Said a boy from Johns Hopkins to Hopkinson Smith,
"Your novels are terribly lacking in myth."
"And yet in my time they considered them topkins,"
Said Hopkinson Smith to the boy from Johns Hop-
    kins.


### AN OLD FAITH FOR NEW NEEDS

Said Reinhold Niebuhr to Nibelung Mime, "S-
ometimes I still get the screaming meemies."
"You've strayed from the worship of Wotan, mein
    lieber,"
Said Nibelung Mime to Reinhold Niebuhr.


### 27, RUE DE FLEURUS

Said Rudolf Steinach to Gertrude Stein,
"As a glandular freak you're all very fine."
"There are those against whom one must soon draw
    the line, ach!"
Said Alice B. Toklas to Rudolf Steinach.


### THE RABBI TURNED AWAY IN DISDAIN

Said Rabbi Ben Ezra to Ezra Pound,
"You can rave all you like, you're not really pro-
    found!"
"My answer is, ἐν δύο τρία τέσσαρα!"
Said Ezra Pound to Rabbi Ben Ezra.

— Or else to imagine History as a crystalline sea-anemone.

# The Pickerel Pond: A Double Pastoral

*Amphisbaenics (backward rhymes)*

## 1948

### I

The lake lies with never a ripple,
A lymph to lave sores from a leper:
    The sand white as salt in an air
    That has filtered and tamed every ray;

Below limpid water, those lissome
Scrolleries scribbled by mussels;
    The floating dropped feathers of gulls;
    A leech like a lengthening slug

That shrinks at a touch, ink and orange;
A child's wrecked Rio Janeiro,
    One fortress of which flies a reed;
    The cleft and quick prints of a deer.

—So, somewhere not far north of Nauset,
Between the girt bay and great ocean,
    It spangles the wrist of the Cape,
    A gem at once clear and opaque.

But the frogs hush their rich jug-o'-rumrum:
From above moves a menacing murmur
    That loudens to shouts, toward the cob-
    alt pond, through low pines and scrub-oak.


Amid laurels and briers, the spider
Winds up, in surprise, then redips,
    To wait at the end of her rope,
    As past down the white path pour


Dogs and people: brisk Scotties, agog;
An old analyst, plodding and gaga,
    Left behind by a bad-tempered chow
    And a bare-footed boy who cries "Ouch!"


At a tree-root but bounds like a leveret—
While his father talks eating and travel,
    With a lady who loves Buda-Pesth
    And knows where they made the best *cêpes*


In unspoiled and unoccupied Paris;
Who has tasted new yam and cane-syrup
    In Haiti, known white vodka-nights
    On the Neva, seen Spain, Palestine,


Nova Zembla, New Zealand and Chile—
While behind bustles Pavel Ilyích,
    Long an exile, who never strikes root
    But lives on continual tour,

234

Amusing, amazing, absurd—
A balletomane coupled in *drúzhba*
   With a David to harp to his Saul,
   Demanding incessant applause:

A sulky and vain young Achilles,
Smooth as silk yet hard-grained as silica.
   A learned Hungarian dwarf,
   Now a foundation-fattened fraud,

Is gallant to old Gladys Doremus,
Who has pleasantly spent every summer
   Since nineteen hundred and ten
   Making turbans and drapes out of net;

While, behind her, thin, waspish and neat as
A pin, in a yellow sateen
   Swim-suit, her prettiness pert
   If wizened, pedantically trips

Her Clarice. She, carrying salad,
Coquets with a young man from Dallas,
   Who majors in French, translates
   Aragon, thinks Valéry stale,

And works for a Stalin committee
And on tennis, at which she can beat him.

235

Dropping off to pick blueberries, lag
Her identical twins, tiny gals,

Whose father has vanished; dim soul of
Devotion, an old setter follows.
   First a dip: now all figures are seen.
   Of the Magyar and Viennese,

One floats on his back like a bobbin,
One squats on the beach like a nabob.
   The boy pushes off a blue raft.
   Overhanding it— Heavens, but far!—

The ladies make Pavel uneasy.
Renowned for her festive cuisine,
   Old Gladys, doggedly gay,
   Hands everyone half a stuffed egg.

They complain about Koestler, Camus;
Take harmless for poisonous sumac
   Till old Gladys's girl sets them right.
   Franz flaunts his Antibes attire,

A bright beachrobe.— "Meatballs or chicken?"—
They talk of Nizhinsky and Nikisch.—
   No knives can be found to carve
   Among flat silver loaded *en vrac,*

So they pull at the drumsticks. A subtle
Sprinkle of dill on lettuce
    With mayonnaise, much admired.
    The Riesling is cool and dry—


Ferenc's gift: "Pliz, pliz—it is nossing!"
The student and traveller, *Gnossen,*
    Are staunch for the Soviet courts.
    The old white dog, with a stroke


Of his tail, overturns a tomato
Sandwich. "I eat automat,"
    Boasts the Bolshevik, picking it up.
    "This is all a big treat."—"Let me put


Some wine in your glass." "*Sposíbo!*"—
A bullfrog, green and obese, hops
    Away from the prod of the sticks
    Of the twins.—The Russians do skits


On opera. An outboard horror
Bears down with a snort and a roar, "Oh,
    Gosh, it will scare all the fish!"
    The boy curses, casting. "*Ein Schiff!*"


Pavel hails it. The chow paws the dirt up,
Having got wind of something putrid.

Gay Gladys hands round the cake,
But nobody wants any cake—

Perhaps a drop more of the white wine.
Chirps Clarice: "On a clear moonlight night I
    Love to walk miles"— "Mama!
    Can we have another ham?"—

"Alone on the sand, like Thoreau.
I imagine the moon-goddess Astoreth"—
    The travelward leer of her beau
    Has made her a xenophobe

As well as a bore, as he tosses
Out "bourgeois" and "yellow dog," says it
    Just makes him fuming to hear
    "Bellyaching from émigrés

Who cleared out and betrayed the masses! "
"That word is your open-sesame—
    Means nossing, unlocks no doors,"
    Declares Ferenc.—The youth is rude.—

"Are the masses Stalíne and Vyshinsky? "
(The twins cry, "No fight, Fergus! Ixnay! "
    Holding a Scottie in leash.)
    Pavel chatters; his dancer, Achille,

Provoked by the epithet "fascist,"
Grows peevish and spits a shaft

That stirs Gladys to say with a smile,
As she proffers gin-fizzes with limes

From a thermos, kept cool by the vacuum:
"Never mind about Miliukóv! "—
    And, pouring out coffee with cognac,
    By a vacuum kept hot: " Oh, can you

Make her tell how she camped with Kirghiz
On the steppes? how she managed to see Greek
    Islands no tourist had trod?
    That archaic lean life, I'd adore it! "

And, relaxed from contentions, efforts,
Frustrations, defeats, trophies,
    Some swim, some take vitamin pills,
    Some walk on the beach, and some sleep.

II

Was I there? Did I share their mild revel?
Did I listen to all their palaver?
    Did I say pleasant things? Did I laugh?
    Many times between April and fall,

Many somnolent hours of sun, a
Comforting muffler upon us,
    While our lame words recurred like this rhyme
    Of wheels that slip round in a mire—

Of boats, tied betimes in a haven,
That lift and that dip and will never
    Put out now to sea, where sleek sharks
    Are circling and steamers crash.

But tonight I come lone and belated—
Foreseeing in every detail,
    And resolved for a day to sidestep,
    My friends and their guests and pets,

Their poses, opinions and gossip;
To try the wild freedom and peace ag-
    ain of this spare little spit
    That beckons with bent finger-tips

To the peaks of the nearest Azore,
As the sun, a dry *vin rosé*,
    Orange-pink, darkens the pines,
    And I startle a pair of snipe,

By the pond's marshy side, from a tussock,
Where their chicks with rich leeches they cosset;
    But I stumble from hummock to hole
    Toward the purple-topped stalks: therebelow,

In search of their prey, my prey lurk. Hip-
deep and hoping for pickerel,
    I peer: there the deeper part stops—
    Here the patching of paler spots

Shows plain as the sunfish's home,
Fin-brushed, where, unflurried, they mosey,
  Gray shapes that glide briefly or stay;
  Hardly moving, the females wait.


Now a weed-stem has twined on my spinner;
Now a faint nibble nips and renips;
  A mudded branch snaps my gut;
  A dull weight that gives at my tug


Turns out, tenaciously shut, a
Damned mussel not worth a tush;
  Now my line springs alive—pull!—it spills
  A slim eel—a quick squirm and he slips


From the bank.—Is this sport? I might tire.
Have I brought the right bait at the right time?
  And as, soundless, I poise with my pole,
  Still casting and cold, on the slope


That dips toward the densening shadow,
Where lumps that loom turtlish or toadish,
  Vague fish-forms, a forest of stem
  And old leaf-mould and slime have met


To melt: the alert, the alive,
Made one with the duller and viler—
  As I paused here, so long have I pored
  At the brink of the mind's dark drop,

Where, below life's articulate noise, you
Feel all in unuttered confusion,
    All fluid, all formless—But what?
    Rod arches and line stretches taut!

A sunfish, flashing, blue dappled
On yellow, gills daubed with bright red, lepid-
    opteral, swings to my reach—
    No sweet prize such as sportsmen cheer,

Yet, emblazoned, with black and gold eyes, a
Splendor that queerly consoles, as I
    Flourish him, suddenly bared,
    Who, suburban by habit, looked drab

Or moved like penumbra on mud-lees
That, neutral and narrow, concealed him—
    As I grasp his strong spines and fat side,
    And detach him before he dies.

So, elliptical, slippery, gemmy,
He rises, unsought—such an image
    As, in hours besotted and soured,
    When it brings no repose to drowse,

Unaccounted-for skims to the retina
From *bas-fonds* not barred by that janitor
    Who guards the true gate of dreams—
    Where dreads with desires are smeared

Upon horrors forgotten since suffered,
Old foods now rejected refuse,
 Out of which appear patterns of lace
 That appal me, and faces assail

My consciousness, smiling or solemn,
That no recognition mellows,
 Always staring, but not at me;
 That, speechless, would push me to scream,

As one ebbs and another brings pressure;
That, plaqued there too clear, usurp
 At once the known drama of day
 And night's not unknown masquerade.

Ah, better my friends than those demons!
These see me and hear me, these know me;
 Like them, I must outlast an exile.
 Yes, liefer their flightiest lies

Than those watchers that fear no revéille,
Whose bodiless heads never waver:
 Girls cat-eyed, not young but smug;
 Gross men that show ugly gums

In a grin that embraces their molars;
Gourds clerklike or salesmanlike, sallow,
 Mustaches kept short, minds applied,
 Eyes cold, self-contained, crocodile,

Gooseberry, grayish or hazel—
Faithful either to outmoded laissez-
    faire or new government rule.
    —No pickerel has lunged to my lure,

As the sky squeezes down its last lemon
And the lake gleams a blacker enamel.
    In this pond of the pan of my skull,
    Where spawned thought should take body, the
       luck's

No better: no bright live elaborate
Sunfish, but only those terrible
    Faces like bubbles in scum
    That pop from the deepest muck;

And, persistent above the blank water,
I, perverse, twist or wrest the retor-
    sion of words—flapping wings that would soar
    Pinning back, spiring tendrils that rose

Training down; tack and turn on a de-
vious route, tracing boustrophédon
    Words that must always withdraw
    From the boundary they labored toward;

Creak a tune darkly dodecatonic
As it cancrizans creeps and cannot
    Be caught; drive a widdershins rout
    That ends in the Dark Tower—

Till, as even the shallows grow dimmer,
As I lose my last live-bait amid
   Mosquitoes that needle a mood
   Masochistic, benumbed by our doom,

All such mutinous music as muttered
Between the bleak spring and mild autumn
   Now but hobbles and stutters, half-dumb:
   Hungry pickerel that nuzzle the mud.

—Gimme the gimmick, Gustave!

—Ah, *that,* my dear fellow, you will have to find out for yourself.

He consulted a typical timing guide, a capital schedule tendency. Excising a light proboscis, he perpended a myriogramme, and added the sum and the quotient. The quotient appeared to be urgent. "A binge that doesn't impinge," he said. The rats ran away by themselves; he prepared to make friends with the beavers. One beaver was full of bravura. He extirpolated a second faking. Now the giddy conked in on his skull. A marginal shrinking and shrieking.

Looking out on the high chalkbound cliffs that take their rise to the north of Seagrom, one made out, on the narrow road that runs below, a woman in a sunbonnet driving a car that was blazoned with a great red A. One was now in the Hawthorne country. In the uplands that lie beyond, one became aware of concealed torrents that hardly relieved the aridity; and a little below Moravia, the lakes and the fractured slopes had almost the look of oases.

# The Rats of Rutland Grange

A CHRISTMAS STORY

I

'Twas Christmas Eve, and all was tense;
The household hung in mute suspense.
Last Christmas night—the memory hurt—
The Rutland rats, so spry, expert,
Audacious and indomitable,
Leaping from floor to chair to table
To mantelpiece, defiant, mocking,
Had rifled every Christmas stocking
Of peppermints and chocolates,
Of almonds, tangerines and dates.
Old Poppa Rat had brought his brood
The doll for little Ermyntrude,
And they had much enjoyed the treat
Of playing with her hands and feet—
Of trying on her dainty dresses
And nibbling off her golden tresses
To taste the rich delicious glue;
They partly ate a shiny shoe;
But carefully preserved the rest
They knew that they could not digest,
And kept it always near the nest.

Now, little Ermyntrude and Mike—
He had not lost his English bike

252

But half a dozen tennis-balls—
Had plugged the breaches in the walls,
Put poison out, constructed traps:
False cupboards closed by falling flaps
(Their fond but cat-allergic father
Had told them firmly he would rather
Not have them bring a mouser in);
But all in vain: the constant din
Of scurrying rats disturbed their sleep:
They'd hear them scrunch  and scratch and leap
To kitchen shelves, where they'd devour
Corn Fluffs and Magic Pancake Flour.
These rats had come to know too well
All death-baits that the druggists sell;
They'd watch the rigging of the traps,
The simple strings and trips and straps,
Then spring them. Keenly they enjoyed
The children's groans to find them void.
They'd sniff the reeking sulphur fumes
That always filled the silent rooms
Where sandwich, cake or canapé
So too ingenuously lay,
And give them a wide berth; and yet
One modern trick they had not met:
That chic and formidable fake
The best exterminators make:
The death-dispensing chocolate cream—
So elegantly shaped they seem
A present for a cozy aunt,
A dainty for a débutante.
Of these our little friends had learned

And bought a box, and now they burned
To try them. Sitting gaily hunched
In bed, pretending greed, they munched
Real chocolates they had mixed with these;
Then, setting on the mantelpiece
The open box, they hung their hose,
Turned out the light, commenced to doze.

## II

Alert, meanwhile, and unafraid,
Old Poppa planned another raid.
Though aging, not yet in the sere,
He still produced five broods a year:
An eager and an agile clan—
Which gathering, he described his plan,
And ended with a lively burst
Of eloquence, not unrehearsed:
"Today our hardy race of rats
Are Rodentry's aristocrats;
And of the race of rats our line
Is supertough and superfine.
Need I recall our ancient claims
On France's oldest noblest names?—
Our work they never can forget,
In dungeon and in oubliette
Of many a medieval château!
We put the bee on Bishop Hatto!
Two ancestors of ours, again,
Attracted the incisive pen
Of Louis's poet, La Fontaine—

Who whisked away the historic egg,
Conveying it a quarter league.
Ah, how we fellows know the knack!—
One clasped it, lying on his back;
The other dragged him like a car—
We'll need that trick tonight—ha ha!
—Heroic in the elder days—
Though Hercules got all the praise—
We slew the fierce Lernæan viper
    By swarming up his several necks.
But those who followed the Pied Piper,
    Ensorcelled by his silly hex—
They were not of our kin or kith.
No question but the tale's a myth."
Then, turning to his favorite daughter,
For whom he'd built a special grotto
Of straw and stuffing from old chairs
Just underneath the attic stairs—
The cream, he thought, of ratty kind,
So shrewd, accomplished and refined:
"The prize, my princess, you inherit
Of long accumulated merit.
Outlasting insolent navies sunk,
Proud palaces collapsed to junk,
Sudden disaster, slow reversal,
    Mammoth and—let us not doubt—man—
All-penetrating, universal,
    We now look back on what a span!
Expand through what a space! we rats
Of English-speaking habitats—
With foreign cousins, Little Missy:

Our German *Ratten*, Russian *krysy*,
Parisian *rats, gros comme ça*,
That go to race at Étretat;
We claim of right the richest spoil
The world can yield; nor need we toil.
Leave labor to these clumsy grubs,
These drudging giants and their cubs!
This house is *ours*—we freely range
The halls and walls of Rutland Grange.
Its present tenants, as we know,
Moved in but seven years ago;
But we arrived when it was new—
I think, in 1882.
What human foot can trace our path?
Our labyrinth of brick and lath
    Would balk a Cretan. Once inside,
With cookies, crystals for the bath
    And other dainties, we'll deride
Their helpless probings and their wrath-
    ful bellowings!—Boys, let's go! " he cried.


### III

Now, Santa Claus has long been old,
The nights he drives are mostly cold;
And yet this Christmas he seems weak.
His reputation past its peak,
He fears the waning of belief.
"The sturdiest faith," he broods, "is brief;
The loveliest legend soon, alas,
Dissolves." He swoops to underpass

A flyer from an Arctic base.
"I'm hardly sure they'd know my face,
These brats that grin at brash buffoons,
Sit rapt by rancid ballad tunes
Projected from far-distant points.
My swift and once breathtaking jaunts
Such stay-at-homes no longer thrill;
    They don't, in fact, I hear, believe them:
    With no equipment to receive them,
They cannot turn me on at will."

Then, dropping toward the slates and gables,
The elm-tops, cupolas and stables
Of Rutland Grange, he mused, "At last,
No ghastly television mast!
This little Ermyntrude and Mike
Old-fashioned presents used to like.
Now let me see what I have got—
A Henty and a Walter Scott;
A box of paints, a game of darts.—
    Aha! a set of anagrams—
They've got beyond the stage of "Hearts"—
    A jar or two of luscious jams."
How happily he nods and beams;
Then notes the box of chocolate creams,
Which puzzles him and gives him pause:
No maker's name. Now, Santa Claus
Knows all the brands from worst to best.
He breaks one, bites it, just to taste
The quality and flavor. "Queer.
I've something better for them here.—

I hope you have been very good,
You little Mike and Ermyntrude,"—
He smiles upon the sleeping pair—
"I've tried to answer every prayer:
*Jo's Boys*, air-rifle, cuckoo-clock,
And battledore and shuttlecock—
With Concord grapes and candy canes
To top them off."

                        But sudden pains
Now grip him. Agonized, he clasps
His corpulence; then, fainting, grasps
The mantel; sinks; unhooks his clothes.
A moment's respite from the throes
Admits a thought that loads despair
On torment. Have the children there
Designed a hoax?—do they, then, scorn him?—
His death, perhaps?—will no one mourn him?
A groan escapes his lips.

                        In fright,
The children wake, switch on the light.
Not only Santa they behold!—
A swarm of rats, bright-eyed and bold,
That vanish quickly—all save one
Who lurks inside the hearth, alone:
'Tis Poppa's clever Little Missy,
Who, quivering her fine vibrissae,
Sits watching. "Water, please!" gasps Santa.
Well Missy knows how parched will pant a
Poor poisoned rat for drink. She slips—
A flash—to Santa's gaping lips,
And, clinging to his whiskered chin,

She darts her delicate tail within,
Applies a light emetic touch.
The Saint makes first a frantic clutch,
Snaps shut his jaws to close the chasm;
Then, shaken by a seismic spasm,
Spews up the poison; now lies still,
Relieved, though queasy—not so ill.

All this was clearly understood
By able little Ermyntrude.
She wakes the household. What a fuss!
"The doctor! You must stay with us! "
"Ah, no, my friends, I cannot stay.
Support me to my waiting sleigh.
So many stockings still! Away! "

Meanwhile our gallant little rat,
Legs shaking, heart gone pit-a-pat,
Along dark galleries dashing, glides
In silence; stops and listens, hides
In terror of remote alarms;
Then finds her worried father's arms.
A look of horror halts his greeting:
"What dreadful thing, my little sweeting! "—
"I know I'm all a nasty mess"—
"Your tail! " he shrieks in shrill distress.
And, glancing round with lifted paws,
She learns, in panic, all her loss.
For, bitten clean by Santa Claus,
That lovely tail, as withy lithe,
With pride to curl, with passion writhe,

Fine-meshed and flexible of scale,
Slim-tapering—poor Missy's tail
Is lopped away. A burst of tears.
Papa, grief-stricken, storms, grows fierce:
"What made you do so mad a thing? "
"I thought," she murmurs, faltering.
—"I hope I'm swift, I hope I'm sly—
I thought we must not let him die."
"What? not to spite those little smarties? "
"But that would spoil our Christmas parties!—
Prevent the pleasure, Father dear,
Of robbing them again next year! "

Was this the truth, this ratty reason?
Or had some vibrance from the season
Of peace, goodwill, to every creature
Resounded in her ratty nature—
Such swift compassion as *we* know
In witnessing another's woe—
To prompt her kindness, at the price
Of what a costly sacrifice!

Next morning, though the skies were ashen,
God's bells gave tongue.
                          In such a fashion,
Confused, convulsive, rather strange,
Did Christmas come to Rutland Grange.

SUPERRAT

# THE WHITE SAND

1950

Slender I saw her stand, stooped a little, her arms
akimbo,
Tall and tapering-limbed, half pigeon-toed on the
sand;

Shy but so sure of her beauty that, bare on the beach
in the sunlight,
Smart as a Paris gown, clothed her from head to
foot;

Eyes drafts of daylight illumined, as noon does a trop-
ical harbor,
Bright with the beams it absorbs, burning miracu-
lous blue,

Bending that quick German kindness, that clearness
of Russian perception:
Birch-dwellers' limpid depth, flood that affirms of
the Rhine.

Slender she moved and slipped in—a water-diviner's
osier:
Tiny diminishing toes, dipping brown head, the
pale skin—

Passing our sunburned sprawlers splashing, with
  scarcely a ripple,
  Plying from little hips, loping a lazy crawl,

Lifting lithe angular arms, as her slow easy-reaching
  strokes fell.
  Touched with delight, I looked, suddenly calmed
  and charmed;

Followed her, floating alone, as she lost herself, fluent
  in fluid—
  White that was balanced by blue—shoulders that
  scarcely shone;

Watched her as, rising, she waded, alighting, a snowy
  egret,
  Stepping on slim heron legs, foreign but unafraid,

Folded her wings, still wet—her quietness made me
  silent—
  Dropped to her knees and smiled, asked for a cig-
  arette.


Silent I long remained while there lingered from
  every meeting
  Grace that turned staleness sweet, peace that re-
  mitted pain,

Shed by blue glance and bland brow, where all that
  was simple was noble;

Nothing subtle, for show; all that was gentle, proud.

These in firm stead would have stood me—a wonder half-dreamed, had they ended
Hardly the murmur of friends meeting for menu food;

Fearing to follow, to love you, these I still kept in departing:
Half-shade of Fragonard bluing the green of a grove;

Song that pours plaintive or gay from Schubert's blue-coated Vienna:
Lindens and lonely men, millers and brooks and May;

Voice of an eager Rostóv, alive in his limitless country
Moist with the smell of the hunt—calling and galloping off—

Metaphors all that must fail me—since shadow must stay for the painter,
Melodies pivot in change, pages repeat their tale.

Style bestowed not by skill only, amazing, may modulate—living,
Flushing and fugitive—flesh on its trellis of bone—

Tune the soft flow of the waistline to deep-throated
  intonations,
  Shape to the high-ribbed face rondures of shoulder
  and breast,

Lighting, perceived, a pure image that pulses, that
  hovers, consoling—
  Brightening, even remote, memory hardly dimmed.


Sands that had darkened I lost them—woods that
  had wasted I left them—
  Rubble and splinters to sift, rocking horizons cross;

Then with the white sands refound you in first days
  of fondness and summer:
  High in our white-walled room, hardly an August
  sound

Brushed to us, buried, embosomed in pale privet-
  blossoms, pink ramblers,
  Quietly stirring or calm; guarded by gables that
  rose

Green from the greenery, marshes beyond, that lay
  rippling and silky,
  Rimmed by the woody low hills, houses white
  cubes cut sharp;

Lunching on sliced delicious cucumbers, roucoucoul-
  ing

Pigeons in eaves, with the cool nimbus of wine
   well-iced.

Noons when our blond boys were playing in sea with-
   out surf, we slumbered,
   Salt-steeped and sun-benumbed, sunk in the sand
   of the bay;

Moments when, moving at leisure, you rose, at once
   lissome and gawky,
   Languid I watched you stalk, blond on the zinc-
   blond sea.

Those were the days when the sun and the sea and
   the wine were a pressure
   Fusing partitions of flesh, forcing new blood to
   run;

Those were the days when I tasted you—tender as
   white osetrína.
   Firm as sea-flavored blin melting in delicate paste,

Mousse of fresh strawberries frozen in smooth inex-
   haustible portions,
   Palpitant pools of borscht creaming rich crimson
   rose,

Cream-stirred kisél that keeps tartness—those were
   the days when I drank you:
   Pétillant Rheims champagne ripened by Rhenish
   art,

Slender long-shouldered hock—those were the days
    when I, feasting,
  Summoned a second guest, shouldered from
    broader stock,

Yellow-haired, blue-eyed blondínka, who, stubborn,
    sure-fingered, sure-footed,
  Pushed at the door still shut, rattled the knob to
    come in.


Blue plates with scalloped gilt edges deployed in the
    plate-racks, disclosing
  Violet, crocus and rose, purple and lemon and red;

Middle room bloomed pinks and blues; pink fuchsias
    bedecked a brick terrace,
  Littered with long summer chairs. Summer was
    brisk and confused:

Sand in the beds—I but brushed you, when brayings
    of radio'd ballgames,
  Bangings of bedroom brawls, had to be heard and
    hushed;

Dogs driven in from the moon and the dust where
    they basked, barking:
  Doors latched and rooms made dark—dumb, we
    subsided soon.

Winter was quiet and bright—with the sea-going
　　throb of the burner,
　　Chekhov read out by turn, stumbling—you lay at
　　night

Slim in your linen sheets, pink-comfortered, propped
　　in plump pillows,
　　Smiling and kind and still, smooth and "Garde-
　　nia"-sweet.

Silence was never a tension nor ever was movement
　　disunion:
　　Climbing October dunes, skirting November fens,

Threading twig-brittle forests—a touch or a word
　　would reach you.
　　Once on a narrow beach, wild as our outer shore

Wintering bleakly, but cozily hidden, hemmed in by
　　the pinewoods,
　　Drowsy with walking and wine, hugging the sun,
　　you dozed;

Drenched from the opposite bank, a shadow that,
　　black and opaque, lay
　　Deeper it seemed than the lake, daunting the mind
　　with its blank,

Toward me, devouring but faceless, advanced till it
　　darkly reflected—

271

Ochre-patched, pallid-streaked—headlong the humped pine-mass,

Marbling with objects seen that menace; then, mirror-wise spreading,
Painting cordovan red, golden and tan and green,

Stabilized, glazing unbroken, a world hardly skimmed by a ripple
Slow as the pulse of sleep—brisker it widened—you woke,

Wakening love, our dear love, that pushed firm on the sand, among writhen
Whitening limbs of no pith—pines on the high bank above

Brushwood and scrub lifted nobler antlers, extending their lofty
Furry and phallic tufts—silver, the molten globe

Spilled on the western ridge—a bird throbbed—I lay in fainting
Pleasure—a purring plane blemished the blue, a midge.


So by the pool of my solitude, gasping in brackish waters,
Lethargies smothering thought, stupors that scarcely brood,

Easily sliding a shade, you showed me the screen of
    appearance,
  Picturing, terraced and clear, station and race and
    trade;

Set me to pore on, unwind it, reweave it, expand its
    dimensions:
  Tessaract-tissue of sense, intellect—two undefined

Others—"love"? "beauty"?—Oh, wonder that held
    me! Oh, image that brightened
  Seasons of barren spite—borne from the summer
    pond!

Pledged to this world you restore, have you passed
    into all with your blessing:
  Orchards and Chekhov and chess, children and bed
    and board?

Pliant, providing, pervading, evasive, decisive in
    vagueness—
  Bowing, you disobey; vanishing, do not fade—

Spirit as fleet as that fairy that flies to men's need in
    the fable,
  Balming the birth-cursed babe—Iris of light and
    air!

Suddenly turning my eyes, I find myself safe in your
    presence,

Rhine-daughter, northern princess, always with fresh surprise—

Dreaming still—hardly believed, half known, hardly there to revisit,
Save as such verses as these features and form may give—

Fresh for me still in its essence, that shore where your high little instep—
Printing white sand, the fair skin—blue-veined and curved, has pressed.

# A NOTE ON THE ELEGIAC
# METER

The elegiac meter of the Greeks and Romans is not necessarily associated with what we mean in English by an elegy. It is even doubtful whether the Greek word from which our word *elegiacs* comes has anything to do with the word from which our word *elegy* comes. The elegiac couplet in Greek and Latin is a dactylic hexameter followed by a shorter line called a "pentameter," though it is not what is usually meant by *pentameter*: it is actually an hexameter with everything except the first syllable lopped off from the third foot and the sixth foot. The classical example in English is Coleridge's useful couplet:

In the Hexameter rises the fountain's silvery
    column;
    In the Pentameter aye falling in melody back.

This meter "makes its first appearance," says C. M. Bowra in *The Oxford Classical Dictionary*, at the end of the eighth century B.C. in Greece. Most of the work of the early elegiac poets is lost, but the meter became popular in Alexandria: the epigrams of the Greek Anthology are mostly in elegiacs. The Alexandrians seem to have refined on the form: the elegiac couplet now must always be self-contained, which was not always the case with the older poets, who sometimes allowed the pentameter to run on into the following verse, and they perfected the balance which gives point to the line. The Romans took over the meter from the Greeks and used it especially for poems of love: Tibullus, Propertius, Ovid. The cadences of these poets and of the poems in the Greek Anthology I have always found peculiarly haunting, and in two of the pieces above—*The Pickerel Pond* and *The White Sand*—I have attempted to transplant them into English. Not that I am by any means the first who has tried to write elegiacs in the non-quantitative verse of a modern language. Goethe and Schiller became quite at home in it: their book of epigrams called *Xenien* is entirely in elegiacs; D'Annunzio wrote his *Elegie Romane* in the nearest equivalent to this meter that the Italian feminine endings make possible (though, for all we know, D'Annunzio's method may come as close to the original effect as does the stressing of the final syllables that bite off the two halves of the pentameter as it is written by the Germans and ourselves); and the meter—though rather rarely—has been attempted in English: by Swinburne in *Hesperia* and *Evening on the Broads*, by Clough in the interludes of *Amours de Voyage* and in two poems called *Elegiacs*. In America, John Hay, evidently imitating the *Xenien*, composed a set of elegiac *Distichs*:

Wisely a woman prefers to a lover a man who neglects her.

This one may love her some day, some day the
    lover may not.

———

What is a first love worth, except to prepare
    for a second?
What does the second love bring? Only regret
    for the first.

———

Pleasant enough it is to hear the world speak of
    your virtues;
But in your secret heart 'tis of your faults you
    are proud.

And one of Edwin Arlington Robinson's finest
poems, *Pasa Thalassa Thalassa*, is composed in
elegiacs:

Smoke that floated and rolled in the twilight
    away from the chimney
Floats and rolls no more. Wheeling and falling,
    instead,
Down with a twittering flash go the smooth and
    inscrutable swallows,
Down to the place made theirs by the cold work
    of the sea.

But when one tries to write the elegiac meter in
English, one finds oneself at once involved in diffi-
culties one might not have expected—difficulties
which Goethe and Schiller do not seem to have had

to face. There is of course the primary problem of
transposing a quantitative and accentual meter into
a purely accentual one; but there is also the resistance
of our language to being made to submit at all to the
movement of dactylic meter. When one tries to write
dactyls in English, they inevitably, as Saintsbury says,
tend to turn into galloping anapaests, which spoil
the calm mood of revery. The two poems of Swin-
burne mentioned above are striking examples of this.
They start out as elegiacs, but they soon run away
into anapaests. Another peculiar problem is how, if
the verse is unrhymed—Swinburne writes quatrains
ABAB—to procure the balance and point of Ovid
and the Greek Anthology. There does exist, how-
ever, a kind of rhyme in Greek and Latin elegiacs.
These poets do often place syllables that match at
the ends of the two halves of the pentameter.
Theognis seems consciously to rhyme πολλοί with
ἐσθλοί (line 369) and Ζεύς with βασιλεύς (1120);
and Mimnermus μοι with μέλοι (in the first cou-
plet of the first of his poems). But what is common,
in both Greek and Latin, is to separate the modifier
from the noun in such a way that the two endings
will rhyme at the ends of the two halves of the line.
The second couplet of this poem of Mimnermus has:

οἷ ' ἥβης ἄνθεα γίγνεται ἀρπαλέα

Ovid is full of these rhymes:

Qui tetigit thalamos praeda novella tuos

Nec dominae teneras appetet ungue genas, etc.

There are six other clear examples of this in forty-four lines (559-602) of the third book of the *Ars Amatoria,* as well as some near-correspondences which would not seem to be unintentional.

In the two pieces included here, I have tried to write elegiacs in English with a structure of concealed rhymes. In *The Pickerel Pond*, I made no attempt to resist the headlong tendency of the language to throw the stress accent forward, and I have printed the two halves of both members of the couplet as if they were themselves couplets, pairing them by backward rhymes. In *The White Sand*, I kept to the dactylic base, printed the lines in the conventional way and invented a crisscross rhyme-scheme, according to which the accented syllable just before the cæsura in the hexameter—the last or next to last, depending upon the word—is rhymed or nearly rhymed with the final word of the penta-meter, while the accented word or syllable of the last foot of the hexameter is rhymed or near-rhymed with the last syllable of the first half of the pentameter. I have even here in some respects departed from the classical model. Though I have made the couplet the unit, I have not conformed to the principle that no couplet may run on into the next, but have returned to Mimnermus and Theognis in occasionally allow-ing it to do so; nor have I always adhered to the rule that the second half of the pentameter must invari-ably contain two dactyls: I have sometimes written trochees instead. It may be noted that, in the poems mentioned above, Goethe, Schiller and John Hay never fail to observe this latter rule, and that Robinson only once betrays it. Clough sticks to it in *Amours de Voyage*, but in the pentameters of the poems which he calls *Elegiacs* he departs from the classical model more widely than I have done.